Stories

From

Heaven

Volume XXXIX

STORIES FROM HEAVEN®
Copyright © 1996 FMK

All rights reserved.
This volume may not be reproduced in whole or in part in any form without written permission from the publishers.
This was done to protect the exact content of all the Teachings and Revelations due to the importance of Them.

First printing 2005
Volume XXXIX
ISBN 1-892957-39-6
Printed in the United States of America

Published By:
The City Of God
Saint Joseph's Hill Of Hope
Post Office Box 1055
Brea, California 92822

www.TheMiracleOfStJoseph.Org

Stories From Heaven

Stories From Heaven

All Revelations are delivered spontaneously and continuously as witnessed by all those present at the time.

Stories From Heaven

purity because it is full of ego and pride in one's self. Skeptics find it an easy out to disclaim truth.

There is no doubt that it takes time for such Phenomena as this Miracle to penetrate even those minds who feel they are capable of discerning such phenomena. We must not be governed by purely another man's determination, but we must understand that logic, sound reasoning and purpose must be the criteria of our Faith in God.

Stories From Heaven

Now in our time, God is once again giving us "teaching stories" through Saint Joseph and His instrument, Mother Frances. Through her, in a quiet, unassuming and genteel way which appears so "natural", mankind is again being taught the purpose of life, and what God expects man to be like in his daily living. People feel hope in these Teachings. Example is being given.

Two major Revelations of significance have been given for us in our day. Our Heavenly Mother is Part of The Divine, and Saint Joseph is truly The Holy Ghost. These should not bring an immediate rejection, but should pique our curiosity and interest.

Our Faith in God is based upon many mysteries. Whether it be The Holy Trinity, the Incarnation of God, or the Holy Eucharist, men strive to understand these, trying to grasp a small glimpse of the beauty of the Truth They Are. These mysteries also pique our imagination and interest. However, even though we know God revealed these mysteries to mankind and we accept them in Faith, they still remain just that, mysteries.

One has only to look at these "Stories From Heaven" to see the value they are, and to feel the hope they instill. No man can logically deny purity of thought when it is so obvious. No man can deny purity in direction, when it is based on sound morals, sound values, sound standards. Do not be blind to truth. Skepticism is for people who are unable to see the truth of a matter or situation, and many times skepticism drowns out

Stories From Heaven

these Teachings will be found in one of the succeeding Volumes of "Stories From Heaven".

In these Revelations the Saints refer to Frances as the "child", the "funnel", the "spoon" and the "instrument". God made her our Spiritual Mother. For many years now, because of this fact, she has been called "Mother Frances", or simply "Mother". Heaven also refers to people of all ages as "children" and emphasizes time and again, this Miracle is for people of all races, all colors and all creeds.

For someone turning the pages of these "Stories From Heaven" for the first time, they will easily recognize the sound logic and sound direction the Messages contain. Mother Frances hears the Words with the ears of her Soul, and repeats them aloud when she is told to do so.

This Teaching Miracle is a direct parallel to the time Our Lord walked the earth. He did not loudly proclaim to everyone, "I am The Son of God." He taught in a quiet manner, simple, extensive, but always detailed in repetitiveness, instilling in those listening what He wanted them to remember. He taught in parables, short, simple stories containing moral lessons. He knew men could more easily understand and remember the point He was trying to make this way. His "teaching stories" pertained to everyday living, practical matters, and how to become a Saint. He gave hope through these stories. He gave example.

Stories From Heaven

PREFACE

These "Stories From Heaven" could not have been given to the world at a more appropriate time than now. The world is in a terrible state of corruption and confusion politically, religiously and socially. Honesty, modesty, genteelness and morality seem to have been eliminated from our way of life, at least in effect if not consciously. However, God has given the world a Miracle it needs.

On July 28, 1967 The Miracle Of Saint Joseph was formally announced to a True Mystic. God has chosen a woman to give us the sound direction, hope and example we need. It is not the first time God has chosen a woman to accomplish His Purpose, always for a specific task in a particular time. This True Mystic for our day is Frances Marie Klug. She resides in Southern California and is a wife, a mother, and a grandmother.

In this Miracle Of Saint Joseph, many Saints have come forth to speak through Frances Klug. These "Stories From Heaven" are just a few of the thousands of Revelations received through her. Very often these Revelations were preceded by extensive Teachings which time and space did not allow us to put in print. However, a few of

AUGUST 12, 2005 AT 2:09 P.M.

SAINT ANTHONY MARY CLARET

"**Y**es, I am Saint Anthony Mary Claret.

There are so Many of Us present, because of the Importance of how The Creator, in the Creation of human beings, directed all things according to what was proper, what was logical, and what would be most satisfying to the mentality of each type, each background, always considering the result must be Heavenly Guided, Heavenly Guarded, and the Purpose for the individuals to return to The Heavenly King.

I know I speak differently, but Many of Us are always present where this *little one* is, and I add to this, where many of you are present, because you see, the time you spend with others is always Important to Us, due to the fact that you live in a time wherein the 'enemy' of The Heavenly Father and human living, human lives, wants *to corrupt* what is so perfect, wants *to destroy* what is so privileged, and wants *to kill* a Portion of how an individual is morally obligated to return to The Creator as 'a *Saint'*.

I could speak hours, endless hours on this Subject; maybe someday I will have to.

Stories From Heaven   1

Always remember, you were created with *'a Portion' of The Creator within you,* and that Gift of Divine Love never leaves you, because It was given as the Protector of your Soul to one day return to from Where It came, and live with The Creator forever and ever; *but the Soul was given a task of protecting the one in whom It was placed.* The Soul does not want to be a victim of weakness, or rash judgments, or disbelief!"

Stories From Heaven

AUGUST 15, 2005 AT 11:58 A.M.

OUR HEAVENLY FATHER

"**I am your Heavenly Father.
Each time I am able to speak openly, verbally, addressing conditions, situations and, of course, My Love, I do it with a desire to one day know that you will be with Me in Another Place, and that what you have to think about regarding your past ways will be one of happiness, joy, contentment, pleasure and thanksgiving.

The world has been blessed abundantly because I have spoken to so many for hundreds of years, allowing them to know I Am In Existence, and *Capable of hearing them speak words that they willed Me to know,* they willed Me to aid them in certain degrees, ways, manners, and for purposes that they willed sometimes for their Soul.

My Words are always different, but I do this to remind you who take Them and who will read Them, that *I Am Ever Present*. Even when it is just your thoughts, I hear all things, I know all things, and I feel comfortable when you do talk to Me in what you call *'prayer'*.

3

So many times when there are several speaking, the joy I feel is boundless, endless, just knowing that the Souls of so many individuals are present and I am receiving through where They are, words of closeness, of understanding, of personal communication, not ignoring Me."

AUGUST 15, 2005 AT 12:30 P.M.

OUR HEAVENLY FATHER

"There are Many of Us present because of the Importance of the time in which you live, and that it is Important for you to understand that the responsibilities you accept when they are helpful to others, or even to one human being, because 'That Portion' of human living, human life that you do not see with the physical eye, is known as 'a Portion' of The Creator, given to each human being, thus giving to it *an innate sensitivity* to what is morally sound, pure, and acceptable to Me, because your Soul is Greater than you know It to be. It is 'That Portion' of you at a time when nothing else of your physical will show representing you to The Divine.

This may be difficult for you to comprehend, but it is Important for you to understand: In the Creation of human life, all things were taken into consideration, thus giving to the physical vision of the body, with the head and the mind, is evident to others who you meet in the human way, but your Soul that will be returned to a Higher Place one day is never seen in the physical form. It is a private Union of Divine Love between you and I. Love is

Stories From Heaven 5

Important, but how you act expresses your devotion to what is morally sound, pure, good.

There are so many things to help you return to from Where your Soul one day was without you. You are loved more than you know. Remember this."

AUGUST 15, 2005 AT 1:03 P.M.

"There are Several of Us present, more than Twelve. *The little one* tries to guess Who We are, but most of the Names Here she would not know.

This **'Gift'** that has been blessed by The Holy Father Himself, The One Who creates all things, in many ways is Present through everything We speak, is evident in the Joy, in responding to a Gift of this Measure, this Degree, this Purpose, that openly speaks of Divine Love for human lives, human living, human goals, human intentions, human actions; the list is endless.

Children must learn about **'This Gift'**, not that It will make them all walk and work in the same measure, but It will give them strength to understand that The Heavenly Father has the ability to speak on Great Subjects, thus allowing others to know that the human mind, the human body, in the creation of it, has many things to look forward to, to be a part of, and also, to lead others in, regarding their Soul.

So many of Us enjoy speaking through **'This Gift'**, because It is a close association with those yet in the living state, thus encouraging them to live a greater span of knowledge, of hope, of interest, of workability for them.

Participation with The Divine cannot be passed over. It must be brought out and spoken about, allowing those yet in the living state to realize that The Door of Heaven does not just close. It allows the Souls to radiate and to instruct and to aid and to perpetuate Divine Role.

I can say no more, because I could speak endlessly on this. ***It is such a Beautiful Gift of Divine Love for Souls.***"

AUGUST 15, 2005 AT 1:34 P.M.

"There are Many of Us present wherever *this little one* is, because there is so much to be learned, so much to be followed, and so many individuals to see ***the Importance of human life as 'a Gift of Divine Love' from The Holy Trinity.***

The world is a place of great worth, because it has given to human lives a place to live and ***to prepare for 'The Goal of Sainthood'.***

That is why it is so Important that this be reminded to a lot of people, all ages, because most do not see it for the beauty of its presence, allowing them to have a place such as this to live on, and to learn so much on so many subjects; also, sharing different degrees of living a daily life with others that they know, or they do not know, but they recognize in them a communication of *being human.*

Believe it or not, this Statement oftentimes gives more strength than is realized. It is the fact that there are others in the living state, living each day in the human way, ***using human life as the means to one day return their Soul, and be called 'a Saint'.***"

AUGUST 15, 2005 AT 2:19 P.M.

SAINT CATHERINE OF SIENA

"**I** am Saint Catherine of Siena.

There are Many of Us present because of the Importance of what you have added to your manner of living, and how you approach being able to deliver to others how you feel about Important situations, conditions, not just openly spiritual, but logically feasible to give to human life, human living, the advantage of understanding purity over impurity, and spirituality over just accepting what is available for you to be part of.

The word *'spirituality'* is not used much, because so many fear it will be put into a pattern of prayer and emotional advancement. This is not so. Spirituality is Important, because it gives to the individual an innate knowledge of separating spirituality from just morality; also, from the daily manner of how you contact or associate with other people.

What I have spoken may be difficult for some to understand why I would place so much Importance on a wording, but I sincerely feel it is important, because *spiritual sensitivity* plays a major role in how an individual thinks, speaks, practices, or associates with other individuals, not in a total prayerful way, but in a respectful order, and a dignified ability to politeness, caring, respect, and acknowledgement that so many things exist that should be addressed in a manner of respect, participation and way.

It may sound strange, My speaking on this Subject, but It has an Important Impact in many lives, because It instills a percentage of the Importance of every factor that a human being is subjected to. ***Dignity is a main factor in every moment, every day you live.***"

AUGUST 16, 2005 AT 10:05 A.M.

"It is of the utmost Importance, *'This Gift'* that has instructed in so many areas on *the Importance of how an individual lives in the human way,* basing morality and purity of the mind on what an individual partakes in, or permits to be a part of, in any dimension of human living.

It is easy to ignore a subject, but many times it is not ignored when it is *foul* or *insulting* to the spirituality of what an individual should understand is Sacred to one's mind, body and Soul.

Hours could be spent on describing each Sacrament that many times is not seen for what It refers to in Its wording.

You live in a time wherein so many of all ages dismiss the *value*, the *reasonability*, and/or the *option* of how they choose words when they are speaking, when they are using their so-called knowledge and putting it into script for others to read, to learn, and to use.

I will close My Words, but I assure you, I will speak again on this Important Subject that thousands, or even millions of human beings ignore, or do not look into the value of what they are speaking — words that could be pleasing only to the devil."

AUGUST 16, 2005 AT 12:05 P.M.

"Yes, there are Many of Us present wherever this *little one* is, but sometimes We make Our Presence more evident to her, in case We want to speak Words of Importance regarding What is Important for the benefit of the Souls that are constantly in need of being taken care of by the one in whom They were placed at the moment of conception.

Ask yourself: Did you think of your Soul today, and did you say a prayer *for* the Soul and *to* the Soul?

Now, please ask yourself: Is this a habit you have given on this Subject because of the Importance of it?

Now: How many other people do you know that keep their Soul available to them in a manner of speech, or just recognition of Its Presence, telling the Soul that you love Them, or they love Them, according to who it is speaking?

I know What I have spoken today is rare to hear, but it is something to think about, because, do not forget, at the moment of your conception, *you were gifted with 'a Portion' of The Creator* that The Creator knew would protect you in more ways than you would understand it to be, because *the Soul, though not evident to your sight or sensitivities, is always there.*

It was ***a Gift to human lives*** in the beginning of the Creation of human life. Remember this. God has never allowed human beings not to have a certain degree of Personal Protection from The Holy Trinity."

AUGUST 16, 2005 AT 12:53 P.M.

There are about Nine of Them here.

"No, there are Eight of Us present. We smile when We say this.

It is always a delight to be present with you all, because in your human way, you please The Heavenly Father in so many ways, and each time that, in your own way, you say to Him, 'Please help Me, Father, to think only how You Will me to think, and please help me pray,' The Father, in His Divine Love, knows so much more than it is understood about Him.

There is no Soul in the living state that He is not aware of. Your time in what you do is important to Him, because He knows the time will come and you will be standing before Him, and He will speak in a private manner regarding how you walked the physical role in service to The Creator that you did not personally know. You heard about Him, and you knew that He was of The Divine Way and was Important in every way.

You live in a time where in some places there is much confusion, because of the mentalities, the attitudes, the understandings, and the beliefs that so many individuals are the custodians of. Some are weak, some are strong, but the sad part mainly, is how they *ignore* The Holy Trinity. So much is taken for granted, and so much totally ignored.

As you walk the path you walk, in union with others like yourself, it is a happiness for Us to see, because it is similar to the time the men walked with The Holy King.

Truth is Important. Belief in A Creator is Important. Understanding that there is a right and a wrong to everything you may think, say or do is Important. Kindness is Important, because it extends to one or more, your sensitivity mentally, socially, morally.

If I had My Way, I would speak hours to you today, because each one here now is important: the way you accept What you are requested to put into print, the way you respond to a possibility that One of Us will speak; The Father blesses you abundantly.

All of Us Saints could speak hours and hours and hours, because We enjoy your company and how you think, but remember one thing: the day will come and your Soul will stand before The Holy King, and your Soul, do not forget, will remember everything that you participated in, you sacrificed for, and the Love you felt that would give you the strength for Sainthood.

I could speak hours, but I have come today to tell you: All the love you show, and all the other good things you help in many ways, it is recorded along with your Soul."

AUGUST 16, 2005 AT 1:25 P.M.

SAINT ALPHONSUS LIGUORI

"**I** am Saint Alphonsus Liguori.

I come to speak today to share with you ***the privilege*** The Father gives, when He allows Us to be called ***'Saint'***.

The world should know this, and more should be understood in how things are spoken, addressing Dignity when Someone is pronounced *'a Saint'*, even when those reading the Name and the word *'Saint'*, do not understand the full scope of what had to be accomplished for this to be put into print, and then the individual having the Title, *'Saint'*.

Throughout the world there are millions and millions and millions of human beings. Rare does any one of them ever think of one day having the Title, *'Saint'*. Why? Because in the human manner of existence, the word *'Saint'* is for someone else, someone who no longer lives and is given a Title of Honor, Dignity, addressing an Important Factor in his or her life.

You live in a time that has been called *'worse than Sodom and Gomorrah'*. You live in a time when not everyone realizes that they should want to be 'a Saint'. They should want to be named 'a Saint' at a time when they no longer walk the living path in the world.

The Purpose, the Reason, and The Divine Source behind Those who earned the Name, *'Saint'*, is not always understood by those who just call the Name in reference to the One they are speaking about.

So much could be spoken on **this Beautiful Gift** that was designed to add Credence, Respect, Honor and Glory to Those who earned the Title, **'Saint'**.

I speak differently, I know, but it is to let you know that All of Us Here in the Heavens cherish the work that you do, and the sincerity in which you do it, because your Soul is happy when you serve in such a thankless way for the Souls that are with you in your time and day.

The Father says, **'I love you all. I bless you, because, you see, as you work to become known as "a Saint", that means that you will be with Me for All Eternity.'**

AUGUST 17, 2005 AT 12:43 P.M.

OUR HEAVENLY FATHER
MANY SAINTS

"I am your Heavenly Father.

I speak this day because of My Sincere Concern regarding the Foundation of your *Faith in The Divine*. I beseech you today, to follow through with this *Gift*. Never deny It, and never harm It in any way, because when you honor The Divine, you gain much Grace, many Graces, and you also gather more attention to how you act, live, and understand *the Importance of The Divine* that many individuals have no concept of.

If someone were to hand you a billion dollars, but then say to you: 'Are you happy? Do you feel that this will support every moment of every day in your time?' Will this give you *Sainthood in The Divine?*

In so many ways, human beings do not understand the Importance of Some Things they are exposed to, and in other things there is no credibility to it morally, mentally, psychologically, physically, only monetarily.

So Many of Us Saints are with individuals that do not see Us. They are not aware of Our Presence with them, but Our Love for their Soul causes Us to stay with them, hoping that they will awaken to the fact that *to be created a human being has a Gift beyond what anything in the world can give them.*

I speak differently, I know, but there are so many individuals in so-called highly learned abilities, understanding, and in places where they are adored for how they act, how they produce quantities of things, not always quality of things.

This Gift of Divine Love was given through *one small voice* a long time ago. It was to encourage hundreds, even thousands of individuals to respect What was being spoken, and the Purpose for What was being spoken was to enlighten their mentalities that all the physical things in the world *could not compare to the Goal* that they were born to one day be an Important Part of, for *'That Portion'* of them that is *'a Portion' of The Creator,* called *'the Soul'.*

All that I have spoken is to encourage, but also to enlighten those who read the Words, to be mindful that, as in human life there are gifts at certain times, there are goals that are important to the mind and to the personal aspects of a human being, but I promise you, there is *no* Goal Higher, *no* Gift Greater than your Soul returning to The Creator *'a Saint'*.

The *Title* comes quickly by so Many Here in the Heavens, because there are so Many Souls Here in the Heavens that are constantly requesting The Father to help more reach that *Precious Goal* that is not just Happiness, but It gives to the Soul a Gift Greater than Words can explain It to be. *It proves that A Creator Exists Physically.*"

AUGUST 17, 2005 AT 1:14 P.M.

MANY SAINTS

"There are always Many of Us where *this little one* is, because We expect her to speak on Important Issues, Considerations, and Facts for the benefit of Souls, that others present will be able to more fully understand that their Soul, listening to Us, oftentimes closes what is called *a dead line* and opens it to Sound Facts.

We All smile when We speak through *this little one*, because of her persistence, insistence, of Facts.

The Father smiles, because We are conscious of every sound that is spoken, because of the Importance of the Words that are being spoken to aid, to ensure, and to permit only Factual Facts.

As We close these Words, We say to those who take the Words, 'Your desire to follow The Father's Will means more to Him than you could understand it to be, because His Love for The Holy Trinity is beyond what the human mentality could ever perceive.'"

AUGUST 17, 2005 AT 2:25 P.M.

"*The little one* says she is not sure of the timing. We All smile at this, because Our Words are so Important to Us and for the benefit of others, that We will not waste time until We complete What We Will you to know.

Throughout the world there are millions of human beings, all using different patterns of living to establish their welfare, their habits, and their manner of living.

I smile when I say these Words, because They lay the Groundwork for most individuals throughout the world. It is important that the Foundation for human living is to base a degree of Sound Faith on morals, on attitude, and how one uses the daily manner of living.

So Many of Us enjoy just watching different individuals change their manner of thinking and/or their practices in what they will to receive through the results of what they think, say and do.

This Gift The Heavenly Father has given to human life. It is a Gift beyond what anything else can be compared to. It is a Gift of Instruction, a Gift of Knowledge, a Gift of Security, and a Gift definitely of Divine Love.

This Gift carries so many Facets capable for human beings to fully understand *the Value* of being created a human being, and

the Goal that an individual is capable of achieving, but the Goal along the way will give so many *Gifts* to the one who follows the Goal, and treats It with love, not anger; hope, not despair.

My Words are being repeated quickly, because there are so Many Here with Me and They would like to speak. I smile at this, because ***This Gift*** is treasured by so Many not in the living state, and yet Many Who lived the human days of living and enjoy the fact that They can conceal what They think, They speak, They practice, They partake in, or They are the creators of.

Always remember: ***You were created for a Purpose and a Goal. It is your privilege to achieve it a thousandfold.*** Remember this, because The Heavenly Father designed What He knew would give you hope, understanding, and Something to work for, Greater than you could ever know."

AUGUST 17, 2005 AT 3:05 P.M.

OUR HEAVENLY MOTHER
MANY SAINTS

"I am your Heavenly Mother.

There are Many of Us present when We know that you desire to put into print Important Words to give strength to those who will read Them, and to aid them in, to more indepthly understanding the Importance of What is meant.

Today there were Many of Us present and We are grateful for it, because in what We heard occur and the degree of sincerity We saw, it gave hope and a deeper understanding regarding what you were capable of doing, and the sincerity that you showed in accomplishing what you saw as Important.

Many of Us Here in the Heavens find a day such as this bears much hope for those in the living state who are working to help others in what they know.

As We close these Words, We All say at one time: *'Thank You, God, for What You have instilled in others at another time.'*"

AUGUST 18, 2005 AT 12:48 P.M.

"There are Several of Us present.

We smile when We hear you speak on what you sense We are all about. As you have a mentality, as you have the *Gift of the senses* within your being, and as you have the *ability to learn so many things*, it is a *Gift* beyond what you really ever understand it to be.

In the Creation of human lives, The Father chooses where an individual will be created and what will be the individual's size, background, and many other things.

It is always happiness to Us when We speak this way because, do not forget, We, too, at one time were created and had to pass through the different places of growing into an adult and learning how to act, to think, and to support Our way of life.

The **Gift of life** is far greater than it is ever seen to be, because each time it occurs, The Father places within it a **Gift** beyond what the mind can perceive.

It is true, many things have been created that have life, and different facets of this living matter has the ability to do many things, but the only Creation that has that *Goal* to one day return to The Creator **'a Portion' of What was placed in it — That is called 'a Soul'.**

There is so much to be learned about this ***Gift of Divine Love***: being able to be created, being able to learn so many things; also, being capable of addressing so many subjects, all different, and all having a meaning, a purpose, a reasonability and a goal.

Always remember: ***You were blessed with 'a Portion' of The Creator within you that nothing else created has the privilege, and that is called 'the Soul'.***"

AUGUST 18, 2005 AT 1:25 P.M.

OUR HEAVENLY FATHER
MANY SAINTS

"I am your Heavenly Father.

There are Many Saints present with you many, many, many times, because it is Important for Them to hear you speak on subject matter that They ordinarily would not hear on occasional times with other individuals.

You live in a time wherein so much has been revealed that, in many ways, aids everyone who hears it, helping them more fully understand the importance of conditions, situations, or materials of many natures that, when they are close to the human body, or are present in the human body, the knowledge of what is occurring is good to know.

I know that speaking in this manner, this descriptive manner, will be difficult for some to comprehend, but it is important to learn about many things that otherwise were just cast away in the winds.

Some reading these Words may wonder why Any of Us Here in the Heavens would talk on subjects such as these, but some times, many times, the subject matter awakens an individual or more, on protection of the physical or the mental conditions of being a human being, and what so many things can cause mentally, physically, or even spiritually to the mind, the body and/or the Soul.

For some, to read these Words will be difficult to handle, but Many of Us Saints are happy to reveal Words that cause some to think differently than they ordinarily would, due to the fact that time, or a situation, or some occurrence that will, in many ways, help the individual be able to remember that it is closely associated with what they should know, or act upon in a more understanding role.

Think about one thing: When you were learning how to count numbers and you practiced, did not the practice help you to be able to use numbers more rapidly, more surely, more practically now that you are older?

Every human being should know that in Divine Love there are so many things that occurred that are spoken about, maybe not at that moment, but the mentality remembers if and when the time is right. God designed all things like this, to help the human rights."

AUGUST 19, 2005 AT 12:37 P.M.

SAINT MARGARET MARY ALACOQUE

"**I** am Saint Margaret Mary Alacoque.

This ***Gift*** that you attend and you are told from so Many Here in the Heavens, about the Importance it is regarding the *way* you live, the *manner* in which you live, and *how you act* in how you live. Some will say, 'Those three words are the same words in effect.' I smile at this, because every human being understands the meaning of a wording, oftentimes not exactly as it was scripted to be.

I speak today with Much Love from The Holy Trinity for *this little one* We All use to repeat Words she does not hear, because We instill Them into her being, her mentality, thus allowing her to repeat What she does not hear.

In ***this Gift of Divine Love*** that is of such Great Importance to the whole world of human life, human living, the *Gift* is to allow thousands, or even millions of human beings, **the Importance of becoming a Saint.**

When We Saints speak, and We deliver Wording that We know can be heard, read, understood in a degree of more indepthly knowing ***it is Important to strive to become 'a Saint'.***

There are Many of Us present wherever *this little one* is, and many times she addresses subjects that are not seen to be from Us, but it is how We are able to talk What We know is Important to speak — Words that someone can understand, even if they think It comes through her love for them, because *wording* in your manner of living is of great importance *but rarely seen as how great it is*, because when you speak, the tone of your voice, the look on your body, your face, tells others more indepthly what you are trying to say, trying to let them know.

 So much can be obtained when you speak words to encourage others, even some you do not know, because a voice is heard, a voice distinguishes what the words mean and how extensively they can produce a change of thinking, a change of understanding.

 I know I speak differently, but it was to awaken the wording that you feel is cast aside. Always remember, that what you speak is heard, and it oftentimes is remembered giving strength or hope; sometimes, a change in one's life.

 I will close now, but as I do, I want you to know that The Father has asked so Many of Us to speak Words that will give strength, not just to those who hear the Words, but those Words that are put into script for others to read.

 I love you. I don't know what more to say at this time."

AUGUST 21, 2005 AT 9:30 A.M.

OUR HEAVENLY FATHER

"I am your Heavenly Father.

This *little one* I use walks a tightrope that many refuse to see as an Important Means and Purpose for the Souls that every human being is gifted with at the moment of his or her conception.

I have spoken like this before, but many times those who hear the Words dismiss what I would term *'the Meaning of Them'*.

There have been many times since the beginning of human living, human practices, human life, wherein even those who understood the logic in what was called Facts, Truths, they automatically ignore the Reasonability of the Definition given to them, to help them more indepthly understand the Value of the Communication that Many of Us gave them.

Today is important, tomorrow and all days, to the living manner of ways, because each human being has the ability to recognize the Logic, the Fact, the Truth, that *just for their existence alone, there has to be a Greater Source of Knowledge, of Purpose, of Reality.*

I, and Many Here with Me, have given clearly, so many Reasonable Terms, awaking all ages, all backgrounds, on the Importance of being a human being, and *what a Gift of Divine Love represents in its existence.*

I come through this *little one* and Many of Us Saints speak, because of the Importance of what a human being is gifted with. The Gift is Greater than what they have named It, because in their decision, they took It lightly, but *every human being has 'a Portion' of Who I Am, What I Am; It is called 'the Soul'.*

I realize that when I call Myself *'I'* when speaking to them, the term is casually understood, due to the fact they have no full concept of Who I Am, What I Am, How I Am. *The Gift of human living is a step to a Greater Source of Living.* No more need be said."

AUGUST 22, 2005 AT 11:11 A.M.

OUR HEAVENLY FATHER

"In My Desire to encourage many to be aware of My Presence, I do it in a way that I know they would trust and follow What I say for them to understand the Importance of being created *'man'*.

I have chosen *one voice*, and I have chosen others who will follow My Will, to be example of It under all conditions of human practices, wills and understanding.

That *'Portion'* in human beings of all degrees of background, *is My Gift of My Divine Love*, strengthening, to aid them fully understand I am available, and I am also present in ways, perhaps difficult to understand to their mentality, in the ways of man, but I assure you, *It is an Act I am able to practice at all times, because of Who I Am.*

In *this Gift* that has become so widespread, announcing openly in Written Words, *Who I Am, and how I Will them to understand*: Today there are millions of human beings, all backgrounds, and yes, many do not look alike, but I know every one of them through *their Soul Who is 'a Portion' of Who I Am, What I Am.* No thoughts escape Me, no words are spoken that I do not know about, because *in each human being there is a Gift of My Divine Love, called 'the Soul'.* The *Soul* communicates with Me when It feels it is necessary.

My Love for human life, living, for human lives, is based on the Importance of what the Future can mean for the *Soul* that every human being is gifted with.

In the Creation of human life, it was designed with many separate portions of it, reasonable in design for how it would be used. It is called *the senses*, but also, each portion of it has a different name, such as the *brain*, the *eyes*, the *body*, the *legs*, even to a *sound* for them to make to communicate. The amount of Gifts instilled are far beyond what is realized, but there is an awareness of every portion of the design of human life, because of the Importance of what it was created for.

I will close now. I could speak hours because of My Love for this *Gift of Mine*. Never forget, with all the Personal Gifts each human life is endowed with, there is also *a Gift of My Divine Love*. It is called *'the Soul'*. It has a Reason, It has a Purpose for every human being created, thus giving to each one a 'Part' of Divine Love and Protection."

AUGUST 22, 2005 AT 12:43 P.M.

"There are Several of Us present because of the privilege it is to be able to join Others in a Gift of Divine Love wherein Messages are put into print, giving strength on Subject Matter that otherwise would not even be thought about as to the degree of Importance that a Subject Matter can be. Some are excellent in morality. Some are very long when it comes to describing conditions, situations, permissions, rejections of certain codes that, perhaps, are of great need.

There are Many of Us Who want this Gift of being able to speak through *a voice*, and have Our Words put into print for others to fully understand certain Subject Matters that human beings depend upon for Their naturalness, but for Their Right in degrees of Logic, Scripture, and many other things. We have used *one small voice* for so many years, because in *this voice,* **We know What We speak will be repeated in the manner We decree Logical, Necessary, and in a State of Love for The Holy Trinity.**

Today, there are thousands of human beings who are committing sin, not all mortal, but just sins that hurt the Soul that is within them, because of an improper statement, action, or word that diminishes the Grace that the Soul could be earning on something different, something spoken with Divine Love in it.

Those who take these Words know the meaning of What is spoken, because as you put into script What you see Logic in and Hope in, but also Dignity, Purpose, you see the Value of Words that most human beings are capable of using, and yet the Words We dictate through *one small voice* get put into script, and hopefully, They are transmitted in many, many places, helping other human beings to learn how to speak personally, and how to deliver hope, how to deliver spirituality, and how to be able to put things in a format that give strength in many ways to those who will read the Words at another time; but also, those who take the Words are being instructed in What is Important for The Divine.

I will close, but as I do, I say, **'Those who serve The Heavenly Father will one day be rewarded for the time they spent, and the love that showed.'"**

AUGUST 22, 2005 AT 1:18 P.M.

"Our Names are too many to mention at this time, but I promise you, We will announce Them when We see it correct, for What We are about to speak is of Importance for the Souls of millions of human beings.

Human beings were created out of Divine Love, The Father Willing to share with living matter and things how Important being *'a Portion' of Divine Love, Divine Way is* to those who share in the prayers, and also, the way of service in other ways, such as dignity, clarity, and putting into words, thanksgiving for All that is received.

I will write more on this later. I will dictate it, but I will close these Words now, because I want you to know *'how close' We All are to where you are, because of this Gift that is so Precious for Souls of millions of human beings.*"

AUGUST 22, 2005 AT 1:35 P.M.

OUR HEAVENLY FATHER
MANY SAINTS

"There are Many of Us present. It is always a privilege to partake in *this Gift of Divine Love*, because there is so much revealed that is revealed in no other place upon the earth.

There are Many of Us Saints, but as I speak, or One of the Others Here speak, We know that there are Others waiting to use Words that We would not use in the same manner that They will use Them.

It is indeed *a Gift of Divine Love* to be able to serve, to aid those yet in the living state to more indepthly understand *what a privilege it is to be born a human being*.

Each time We are requested to speak through *this Gift of Divine Love*, Many of Us gather because it is of such Great Importance to hear What The Father Wills to be known by those yet who live in the living state, and should more fully understand that it is a *privilege* to hear What they hear, and to be able to follow Divine Plan in the order that It is directed to be, and that is to use every motion of it in prayer and in thanksgiving.

I am your Heavenly Father. It is a privilege to be with you on this day, because there are so Many Here in the Heavens that want your Souls to be returned Here at a time when it is agreed upon, *in the perfect way*.

So Many Saints Here in the Heavens want to bless you all the time, to give you the strength to understand that living the life of a human being is a *Gift* Far Greater than it is ever seen to be, because as you walk in the human role, you have so much to use: you have the *senses* you were born with, you have the *mentality* that can grow into an ultimate source, force, meaning, helping you to more fully understand *what a Precious Gift human life is in so many ways, and for so many reasons, and for the Purpose that was drawn up by Divine Plan.*

I will close, and All of Us Who talk will listen to what you have to say when you read these Words that were given to you to let you know you are not alone in the world, but you are part of a Great Way."

AUGUST 23, 2005 AT 12:35 P.M.

MANY SAINTS

"There are Many of Us present because of the Importance of What The Father Wills to be spoken about, to be understood, and for all to be aware of.

A Word may change the life of a human being, based on their understanding, their thinking, their devotion, and how they face each day mentally, socially, physically.

We speak so many Words through *this little one*, because We know that in her love for The Divine, she would not want you to miss What We have to say, because she knows that We would only speak to aid you, to consider how important you are, and what you will follow, because of the Soul you are in knowledge of, that you are the custodian of.

Too many individuals outside this area where you are, they do not always think of speaking to a Saint, speaking to The Creator just in personal conversation, but I assure you, you are heard, you are felt, and there are hundreds, thousands of Saints Who enjoy the communication, even though it is obviously one-sided; but then, do not forget, when you have the trust, the hope and the love in knowing that when you speak to a Saint, the Saint will respond to you in a way perhaps you cannot see or hear, but *you know that the Saint is aware of what you spoke quietly, or verbally, or hopefully.*

Your Faith is based on Divine Love. No greater love exists in the whole of creation. Divine Love has Faith, Strength, Hope, Encouragement. The list is endless, because The Father, in Divine Love, uses this Love to help those in the human state."

AUGUST 23, 2005 AT 1:07 P.M.

MANY SAINTS

"There are Many of Us present.

The Father smiles because We are so anxious to speak, helping those in the living state to be more able to see the importance of how they live, how they think, and how they communicate with others like themselves.

In the beginning of the creation of human lives so much was taken into not just *Consideration*, but with *Sincere Care*, because in the *Design* The Father Willed human lives to be, much was emphasized on the importance of speech, the importance of memory, and then the importance of the capabilities, physically, that would be necessary to be reached.

So much Divine Love considered every step of the way, because of why human beings would be created, because when The Father smiled and said the creations will be a beauty to see, a wonder to know, and definitely bear the *will* of one day returning *'That Portion'* of them, the **Soul**, to from Where It came, it is so important for all ages to understand that to be a human being is not something in demand. **It is a Gift of Divine Love,** and **the Soul** is to one day return to The Creator, representing the one in whom It was placed at another time.

Though you cannot see the Soul or hear the Soul or touch the Soul, It is always present, because It is 'That Portion' of Divine Will, Divine Love, that connects the beauty, the glory of the human state with Divine Ways, Understanding, and Goal.

We have shown *the little one* how important this is, because It is Greater than It is known or seen to be. **The Soul of a human being is 'a Portion' of The Creator of All Things,** and that is why It must be cared for in many ways: morally, mentally, sensually, spiritually. The list is endless.

Remember, each day you walk in the human way, you are the custodian of 'a Portion' of The Creator. The Name is simple. It is called 'a Soul'. Remember these Words, and when you do, thank The Father for this Gift of His Divine Love that He shared with you."

AUGUST 23, 2005 AT 1:43 P.M.

"**I** am Saint Alphonsus Liguori.

And I am going to surprise you when I tell you how a long time ago I was known as Padre Pio.

I am Saint Francis of Assisi. *The little one* was named after Me a long time ago.

I am Saint Bernadette. I have spoken many times through *this little one*.

I am Saint Margaret Mary Alacoque. We are All familiar with who she is, what she is, and her love for The Divine.

You live in a time that could be, and can be, termed *a Great Time* in the history of human life, human living, human purpose, human goals. You live in a time when so much has been revealed, after a very long time when very little was revealed because of the control that was shown over wording, over association with someone like *this little one,* who has always walked a tightrope designed by those who could be envious, jealous, or cruel.

Today, as Many of Us speak, it is to make those close to her aware of times, oftentimes change, due to how individuals partake in how they think, how they live, and what they enjoy mentally, morally, psychologically.

My Words are different, because it is important that all facets of living human ways, human intentions, human purposes, human abilities, and also morality, moral issues, that must be seen over and above what is just wording to appease rather than please.

We will close these Words, but We do it reluctantly, because there is so much to be considered on *a Gift of such Worth*: the beauty of learning more about The Divine, and the chance to partake in being a part of What will make others see *the Great Worth in All that is Spoken, and All that is a Way to The Divine.*"

AUGUST 23, 2005 AT 2:16 P.M.

MANY SAINTS

"There are Many of Us present wherever *this little one* is, because when she was chosen to walk a path of such Great Importance, there were Others appointed to be with her and to give her help whenever it is needed.

To speak words to the average person is a simple task, but to speak Words you do not think, and repeat What Others say without a sound, because the Words are instilled into the mentality the Speaker's Way, **This Gift of Divine Love is a Gift** beyond what It is seen or understood to be, because there is so much for human beings of all ages, to be logically associated with **a Gift of this Importance** at a time that, throughout the world, has many wrong things. Most of the things that are in this way are not seen for what they really are, because it is innate in human beings to try to *ignore* what is displeasing, and most try to put it in a better way, even if they have to change a few words to make it to be more important, also nicer to hear or say.

Throughout the world there are millions of human beings, all with different IQ's, all with different imaginations, impulses, or all with spiritual manners, way. The list is endless on all things that a human being is capable of being like, or participating in. When I say, *'being like'*, it means personality, backgrounds, nature, or mentalities, in what degree the mentality is. The Words are endless on this.

All the things that pertain to a human's life are Important because of **the Soul** that is not just the custodian of certain things, but *the victim* of a lot of things that a human being considers thinking, speaking, acting on, or morally accepting.

Morals are a very important part of all ages of human living, but so many times it is ignored, saying, *'It is my age,'* or *'It is how I know things to be,'* or many other excuses ringing bells, or accepting the wrong choices to not be ignored, but to be accepted personally.

There are so many things that a human being is subjected to, and it would be better if they cast it aside, but the human mentality has *pride*. ***I beseech you, never allow pride to make decisions for you, but do allow your love for The Creator, your love for The Divine, and your love to enter the Kingdom of Heaven with a Title 'Saint'. It will take a lot of changing in many individuals, but I promise you, it is worthwhile."***

AUGUST 23, 2005 AT 4:04 P.M.

OUR HEAVENLY FATHER

"I am your Heavenly Father.

It is such a delight to have happiness when you see certain individuals enjoying their time and their subject matter that they are involved in, due to the fact that they are happy to be working for a *Cause* Greater than even they realize. The *Cause* is to save Souls; hopefully, thousands and/or even millions of human beings.

Today as I speak, it is because of My Love for this act, this action, and this intention of so many individuals that will automatically extend to a great number; more than is accountable, more are accountable, for What they deliver to others.

If I were to say to you, *'I bless you for what you have accepted, also the work that you are participating in,* to make what you have accepted an important issue, fact, and a personal gift, wanting all who partake in It to be assured that when one serves The Divine, The Divine never forgets, though All of Us Here in the Heavens have different situations, conditions, that appeal to Us because of Our interests in them, and the reasonability that Each of Us cares for different facts, figures, or Acts of Love that others allow themselves to partake in.'

There are so many Words I could speak on this day, Words inconceivable in number, but I assure you, as you practice love for The Divine in the manner you are doing, plus your love for the Souls of other human beings, your love is more than a credit to you. It is a thanksgiving, because you are using your time, your energy, your knowledge, your beliefs, and your love for The Holy Trinity.

You can do nothing that is not seen. You can speak nothing that is not heard. Remember this, because your very presence speaks what you are, who you are, and how you use your time to grow in deeper love, deeper service for The Divine."

AUGUST 24, 2005 AT 11:33 A.M.

OUR HEAVENLY FATHER

"I am your Heavenly Father.

I am aware you live in a time wherein there are many wrong attitudes, understandings, beliefs, and truths that in many ways are liable to how you live and the purpose for which you are a human being.

The Goal that you strive for should be the *Goal* that will return you to Where I am, for a given time and for a time to bless your Soul for how you lived the human way amongst thousands of human beings who, within them, *all had 'a Portion' of Who I Am, What I Am.*

Through *one small body, one small voice,* I have designed *a means to be able to communicate* because of the Souls that are at stake when impurities or wrong, unjust situations, conditions or wording plays a major part, thus causing the Souls a difficult time, and also much hurt.

I speak through *one small voice* that I have used for many, many years, because What I have to say is Important, and it would not be fair on My Part to not allow those in the living state to not know What is occurring and What is beneficial for them, to them, in them, at this time in which they walk, they speak, they learn, and they respect how they feel.

I could speak hours without stop, but I know *the little one* is preparing for a Very Important Step in *this Gift* I have placed within her, to be strong and committed to What I Will others to be helped with.

As I close, I say, *'Those who desire to be blessed gives Me happiness beyond what I can speak in the human way.'* It is important that each day of life should have what is called *'growth'* spiritually, morally, mentally, psychologically, using the human degree of understanding, *because there is a Soul at stake.*

I will close, but as I do, always remember: I love you, and My Love is beyond what you know love to be, because, do not forget, every Soul that has the privilege to live in a manner unseen, *the Soul looks forward to returning to The Creator in a Higher Being.*"

AUGUST 24, 2005 AT 12:48 P.M.

OUR HEAVENLY FATHER
MANY SAINTS

"I am your Heavenly Father.

This Gift of Divine Love in which so much is being released regarding the Importance of the Souls that are dependent upon those in whom They were placed, the Souls are grateful for *this Gift*, because the fact that They are known to be present is important to Them, because the one in whom They are, oftentimes thinks more sensitively and in earnest over helping Them, or caring about Them, or thanking Them for favors they received.

So many human beings are unaware of *a Gift of this Nature*, because they cannot comprehend the closeness It would have, It would be, or all that It would strengthen in the individual; basically, because they do not hear It in a soundful manner.

I could speak hours on this Beautiful Subject, because It is a Gift greater than It is seen to be. *The Father, in His Creation of human lives, thought of everything.*

When a child is about to be made a human member, a human infant, it is such a joy to hear about and to see it occur, because in this Gift that allows human beings the privilege to be the ones in whom another human being is created, is many times far beyond the basic understanding of *what a privilege this is* to the human manner, way of living.

Then, one day a child is born and it draws a lot of attention, because at this point the child has a beginning, to grow in the human way to one day become an adult human being. The time may be rather long because of the timing necessary for the child to grow in the state of all the facts and all the gifts that is, in many ways, so necessary for the child to be able to be a human living being.

I know We Saints do not speak often on this, but there is so much to be thankful for; also, in the responsibility of giving birth to a child, it is giving to The Creator of All Things, an Act of Love greater than it is known or seen to be, because through this birth and the time that this birth will spend growing, learning, and being a major part of the human element that was designed a long time ago by The Creator of All Things, because through human life the Souls have a place to live internally, so one day when the life of the human part no longer exists, the Soul is gifted with the possibility, or I should say, the reliability of the one in whom It was placed; that is, to become *'a Saint'* with the Name of the one They walked in at another time.

  I could speak endlessly on this *Gift* that is not always seen as to what a Major Factor It is to the one that bears the Gift, the one who has the Gift to provide the Gift.

  I know I am going to surprise you with My next Words: Many times when this occurs, sometimes Here in the Heavens there is so much happiness that, believe it or not, there are tears of thanksgiving to The Creator, to see this, to know it, because of the Importance of it, proving that The Creator loves you."

AUGUST 24, 2005 AT 1:15 P.M.

MANY SAINTS

There are Five or Six of Them.

"No, there are Seven of Us Here. We are All Saints with a Beautiful Gift of speaking, being able to speak the Words clearly enough to be understood, due to the Importance of Them when We talk to you.

Ask yourself: How much could you repeat if you were to hear a story of great measure, and the story was so full of facts, so interesting, but rapidly spoken? Logic would tell you that you would have to ask them to slow down.

We All smile at this Statement, because that is why, oftentimes, when We speak through *this Gift,* We slow down so you will be able to hear What We were requested to speak about, because you see, **The Father, in His Love for you, wants you to be able to understand so much more by hearing the Saints speak through 'this Gift of Divine Plan'**, thus, in many ways strengthening your understanding and your desire to learn more, because of What is spoken by the Saints.

When a Saint speaks and you are requested to put It into script, what a Treasure it is, to remind you that you are an instrument of allowing this to be done so others could read the Words that were given, instructing on some Facet of Divine Love, or *for you to more fully understand what a Treasure your Soul is to you,* because Divine Plan constantly and consistently instructs you."

AUGUST 25, 2005 AT 10:55 A.M.

OUR HEAVENLY FATHER

"I have given to the world *Words* I sincerely feel will help thousands of human beings to become aware that I am present wherever they are, and I care, because there is no human being, human life, that does not have *a Goal* to reach at a later time.

It is Important that All I deliver to be put into script, is of the Greatest Importance for all ages of human living, to be aware of the communication that is available for every human being to be able to think, speak, follow and live a life of communication with Me.

No living mentality can fully discern Who I Am, and the Power that is within Me to do all I Will to be done. No mentality has this degree that it would take to understand All I Am, and All I Can Do.

I speak slowly through *one small voice*, because I have requested My Communication with her to be delivered, so others will have the chance to understand they are never without My being able to communicate with them, or them with Me.

What appears as silence on My Part has a Purpose beyond what I can explain openly, but there is no word spoken My Way that I do not know about it.

I could speak endlessly on this Beautiful Association I have with you, and you have with Me. My Love for this Creation of Mine is beyond what It can be discerned to be."

AUGUST 25, 2005 AT 12:27 P.M.

MANY SAINTS

"All of Us thank you all for taking your time to help Us deliver to others, **Messages from The Divine**. We smile when We say, 'We are sorry to interfere with your manner of doing things, but We know that if We enter your presence, you will be kind enough to give Us your time.'

Throughout the world there are millions of human beings that would feel that Our Presence was Important, but they are not instructed how We are given the privilege to speak to an individual, and sometimes it is even passed over, thinking it could not be.

Today as We gather to speak, We felt you should know how We think, because each time We are requested to give a Message, it is Our Duty, Our Pleasure, and Our Love for The Holy Trinity, that What We are told to speak gives strength to numerous individuals who read the Words and apply Them to their manner of living, or to help others know What We spoke about.

There are thousands of men, women and children that would be delighted to know **'how close' We are to them**, but it would not be feasible for them to be told, because there are only certain individuals who We feel will comply with what is needed, and who will contribute their time and their effort so that others will be able to read Our Words, and hopefully, It will give them Innate Directions for the benefit of their Souls, and plus, What they teach to others for their Souls.

When the Word *'Soul'* is spoken, it oftentimes throws some imaginations out of character, because they cannot understand the Meaning of What a Soul Is to them. They have heard the word, but cannot see a body or hear the sound of what the Soul is giving to a particular individual.

I smile when I say My next Words: The *one* receiving the Words rarely hears a sound. The Words are implanted into the mentality, and into the assistance of the *one* chosen to receive What We request them to know. If there had to be sound from Us, it would not be in keeping with how We live, how We speak, or how you would be able to repeat What We would say.

Now, if certain individuals read What I have, or I should say, We have just spoken, they will find it difficult to believe; but nonetheless, These are Facts, and I promise you, It is based on Divine Love from The Holy Trinity."

AUGUST 25, 2005 AT 1:20 P.M.

"We are always present wherever *this little one* is, because she has been given the responsibilities of looking Our Way to check to see if Our Presence is ready to speak Words The Father Wills for Us to say.

You live in a time when there are so many individuals who, in many ways, want to feel important, want to feel they know many things, and yet in the reality of hearing what they have to say, or what they have to show in how they act, is not always beneficial to others in the spiritual way.

I know these Words may offend some, but They shouldn't offend anyone taking Them. It is just to help you be aware that it is important in how an individual speaks, how they express how they think, and also, what they follow morally, mentally, psychologically, spiritually, physically.

Sometimes it is so easy to talk about a subject that someone feels is interesting to those listening, but this is not always the case. Sometimes very Important Statements are made, but everyone present does not understand the full meaning. Now remember, I said *'the full meaning'*, because wording has a way of pointing to a subject matter and then declaring what the subject matter is responsible for, or beneficial to some portion of the living state.

Today when I speak these Words, I know that it could be difficult to understand why I would say What I say, but I beseech you to understand **that *to be created a human being has so many facets to it***: some are beneficial; some are just applicable to the personality of a person, or the nature, or pleasing to the characteristics that an individual is happy to practice, to show to others.

You live in a time when so many human beings enjoy being popular and enjoy being the attention-getter on certain subjects. These types of times have been since the beginning of human creation, but it is important, because it gives sometimes, hope; also, the ability to express one's emotions, one's concepts of understanding, and one's feeling for others present that could not be seen unless the acts or actions were prevalent.

To be a human being has many assets. The Greatest asset, of course, is the fact that **there is a Goal for the Soul of every human being.** This gives much more Importance to an individual when they realize that **the Goal is of Greatness**, the Goal is for the Future of how they will exist according to Divine Will.

Needless to say, I could speak hours on this Subject, because it is interesting, even fascinating, because it helps the mentality, it gives strength in some areas, and it has something to do that could use the time of day more enjoyably.

As I close, I beseech you, as you read these Words, remember when We Saints speak of different Subject Matter, different degrees of how you can be, how you can live, what you can think, what you can say, always remember it is because there are so many *Gifts* in human living that can be good for the mentality, for one's desire to enjoy certain facets of subject matter; but ***always remember, you have the ability to speak to The Heavenly Ones every moment of every day, and this will be a communicative time with Them that one day will be returned to you in a very loving way.***"

AUGUST 25, 2005 AT 2:43 P.M.

SAINT CATHERINE OF SIENA

Is there a Saint Catherine of Siena? She is smiling. She says:

"Yes, you have come upon Who I Am.

There are so many ways, so many times that All of Us Saints Here would like to speak on a one-to-one basis with all those yet in the living state. The Father did not make it to be this way, but We All understand His Caring and His Love for the human race, whether they are in the living state, or in the state of what is called 'death'.

I speak this way, because in having lived the human way in many, many ways, degrees of ambition, consideration, and living with other individuals that all had habits and all were able to speak the words in the manner, degree and way they were used to speaking, it was always a joy to hear someone say, *'Good morning,'* and then at another time, *'Good night; see you on the morrow.'*

You live in a time that is precious in many ways, because there are so Many Saints in the Heavens Who enjoy when They hear you say nice things about others that you work with every day, and the hope you have when you pray.

The time has come for children to learn the Words that give them the Communication that helps them know about the Saints.

You live in a time wherein so many individuals have the desire to do many things, to conquer many subjects, many objects, and many wrong things that should go another way.

Today is always a wonderful time to speak from The Divine, because We say this every day, I promise you. It is Important for Us to share Our Time with all who are yet in the living state, because We see things in a different light, and sometimes when We speak, it is just to have a companionable happy moment from The Divine.

A lot of individuals will not understand My speaking in this manner and way, but I requested The Father to tell Me if I could speak today to those who I knew, who I know, and who I remember as they, too, working to become Saints."

AUGUST 25, 2005 AT 3:17 P.M.

OUR HEAVENLY MOTHER

"I am your Heavenly Mother.

There are so many things I could speak to you on this day, because *this Gift*, designed by The Creator, is *a Gift Far Beyond what It is understood to be*. The Personal Communication given to all who walk the living role, the human role, is a Gift beyond what It can be understood to be, because the Power that radiates through *this little one* who hears Everything The Father Wills her to hear, her position in His Honor, is to speak What He Wants others to feel strength from, hope in, and a Goal for time to come, to one day return to Him and be called *'a Saint'*.

I close these Words, but always remember, I am always one little word between you and I, and as this is so small in dimension, remember: *I am present to hear what you have to say to Me, and I love to hear your manner of prayer, and also when you say, 'I love You, Mother, thank You for All You do for Me.'"*

AUGUST 26, 2005 AT 12:00 NOON

OUR HEAVENLY FATHER

"I am your Heavenly Father.

Each time I walk where you are, I immediately want to give the Words to you that I desire thousands of human beings to know.

You live in a time wherein there are many things occurring that are diabolical by nature, and hazardous to the human being.

As I speak these Words, I speak Them with much Concern, because every human being created has *'a Portion'* in them of *Who I Am, What I Am*. Human life was designed in this manner, this way, because human life was to be given so many *Gifts* of understanding based on morality in the true sense of what the word means: *purity of the heart, the mind and the body; justice in every fraction of human living.*

The Words are endless, because you see, there is a Place in Heaven for every human being created, and this Place is What should be the *Goal* for all ages to think about, because each human being is gifted with *a Soul; a Soul, 'a Portion' of Who I Am, What I Am*. That is why human living, human life has so much foundation for it to more fully understand, it is Important to reach for *the Goal of Sainthood*.

I smile when I say My next Word: 'Amen.'"

AUGUST 26, 2005 AT 12:34 P.M.

"There are always Many of Us present as We All communicate through this *one small voice*. We All smile each time We are beckoned to be able to be alert, so when the reading starts, We will be sure to have the Words.

Today is an Important day, because We are aware of certain individuals that are using this day to become more acquainted, more understanding regarding **this Gift of Divine Love.**

There are thousands and thousands of Words yet to be spoken to aid the mentalities of hundreds and hundreds of people, because of the Importance of What is being delivered through *one small voice*, encouraging many ages of human beings to be more alert to how they think, what they learn, and how they practice what they know would be good for them to follow, in their manner of living and in their desire to please The Holy Trinity in a greater degree.

So many times when a human being, of any age, learns that **there is a Greater Entity of Divine Love** than they have ever seen, it gives them strength, it gives them hope, but it also encourages them to practice more, in many ways, wanting The Divine to recognize them based on humility.

I will not use many more Words because I would like to speak hours on end regarding this Subject Matter.

Be blessed by What you feel, be alert by What you feel, and never forget: ***The Father is always present wherever you are, so you can say a prayer anytime you desire. Remember this.***"

AUGUST 26, 2005 AT 1:00 P.M.

OUR HEAVENLY FATHER
OUR HEAVENLY MOTHER
MANY SAINTS

"There are Many of Us present. The list is endless because of the Importance that Each One Here wants to speak about.

This *'Gift'* has been given to the world through *one small voice*. Dignity, Purpose, Reasonability and Hope are the Foundations many times that *the little one* encourages Us to speak. We All smile, because her love for human life is greater than it is ever seen to be, and needless to say, her love for Us is based on The Holy Trinity.

There are thousands of Words that could bespeak the Importance of living the daily life as a human being. So much would have to be spoken in detail for some to fully understand, but as We come today to speak through *this small voice*, We know that those taking the Words will feel Our Presence, and also the necessity for What We have to say.

Each human being knows purity from impurity, justice from injustice, hope from despair, love from hate. These Words are endless in what They mean, because every human born is gifted with *a Soul* that nothing else created has.

So, let Us start now in a softer way, because of the Importance of every day that is lived, and there are many challenges to it, many decisions to be made.

I, your Father, love you. Never forget this.

I, your Heavenly Mother, love you. You can be sure of this.

We have given this 'Blessing' to *a little one* We knew would be cautious, careful, and thorough in how she would produce What We Willed you to know, to learn, and to have, to give you the strength to follow Divine Will, Divine Love, over and above any other thing that might draw you away and not give you the strength to pray when you know it should be, and to speak personally, helping you to communicate.

You live in a world wherein there are many things occurring, but really always have, that are not morally sound, morally pure, morally clean, but each human being has been given *the ability to choose* and then to speak, thus allowing themselves to choose what is pure, just, correct, not just practical, but all the things that help the Soul in many ways.

Think about this. There are some times in one's life when they feel they need someone to care, someone to help them, someone to share; maybe it is a pain somewhere in the body, or a sorrow mentally. Sometimes the easiest help you can receive is by kneeling down and asking The Creator to give you the strength to persevere, to be able to handle what is necessary to accomplish what is needed.

I could speak hours on Divine Love for the human living, because in the Creation of human life, The Father considered all facets in how it would adjust to many things, many ways, many conditions, many decisions; plus, knowing that much depended on the degree of understanding and love for The Divine that things were based on.

I will close My Words at this time, but I am sincerely grateful for the time I have been able to say these Words, because All the Saints in Heaven love *this Miracle*, and They want those who partake in It, to remember *this Gift was given to awaken some, to encourage some, and to aid some in remembering they have been given the Love of The Divine that is called 'a Soul', that one day is to return to Heaven.*"

AUGUST 26, 2005 AT 1:55 P.M.

"So many times when We speak, We know there are many who find it difficult when We mention Our Name, because they are not aware of Who We are, or What We are all about.

Throughout the world there are millions of human beings who do not understand **The Holy Trinity**, nor do they understand that as they were created in the human manner, way, for a Purpose, they oftentimes ignore what the Purpose is, because they look more for the materialistic practices they associate with living the life of a human being.

I could speak hours on this Subject, because it is a Subject that is daily abused by thousands of human beings, because they feel that their thinking is more practical and more apt to be what would be wanted by The Holy Trinity.

Those who read these Words will see what sadness it can be, when there is misinterpretation of any gift to The Holy Trinity."

AUGUST 28, 2005 AT 9:32 A.M.

"This *little one* is the *victim* of an unseen entity that is and was initiated by envy, jealousy, and widespread hate. It is so easy to accept what only pleases the personal ambitions, intentions, and desires to be great.

You live in a time wherein so many human beings do not see the Importance of being created a human being. ***The 'Goal for the Soul' is rarely understood as being 'a Major Portion' of being created a human being.***

We hear many think on *their interpretation* of their creation, thus ignoring what **a Special Gift human life is**, due to the fact that it bears within it **'a Portion' of Divine Love** that rarely is thought about as **the Great Gift It is.**

There are Many Saints that want so much to speak in a manner and way, easy and logical to understand *what a Gift human life is to man.* The *Gifts* of human living should alert in each mentality, the very fact of the structure of human living, of human life, and the physical, in capabilities it is endowed with, in.

I could speak hours on this time with you, because it is important for thousands, or millions of all ages of human lives, to more readily and fully understand the *Gifts* of living a human way were based on what The Creator had, thus allowing human life to see, to feel, and to understand it was not just created to please Divine Plan, but there is *a Goal* for *a Portion* of it to one day be returned to The Divine forever and ever, in service beyond what the human mind can perceive it to be.

Human life, bearing the ability to do so many things, is a *Gift* Greater than it is seen to be, understood to be. It was created as *the foundation for one day to be with The Holy Trinity, in Service, in Honor, and Divine Love. Nothing else created has this Gift, this Personal Association. Remember this.*"

AUGUST 29, 2005 AT 11:00 A.M.

OUR HEAVENLY FATHER

"I am your Heavenly Father.

The Gift of human life has many purposes. Basically, it is to use the life to grow in more understanding of *the Purpose for human life* and *the Goal awaiting it* at a given time, for the rest of time.

So many individuals find this Statement difficult, because they do not see the Importance of human life in a living state, and then human life meeting The One Who created it as a Blessing for the sake of *the Soul that will remain forever*.

The little one I speak through is much more sensitive than known to be or expected to be, or understood to be. When We speak, delivering to her Words that no one else can hear, We hand to her a responsibility Greater than It is ever seen or thought to be.

Prayer is of the Greatest Importance in all human beings, because of the subject matter it speaks, not just acknowledging the Beautiful Purpose of it, but instilling the *Goal* it was created to reach; thus giving to the one who is oftentimes speaking or delivering, but it

is a Blessing for the Souls Who hear it and are many times aided through its words.

I will close, but as I do I remind those who read these Words *to cherish the life of the human way*, and *be thankful for the many Gifts*, and also the *Goal* it was created for: *to one day return as 'a Saint'*."

AUGUST 29, 2005 AT 12:05 P.M.

OUR HEAVENLY FATHER

"I am your Heavenly Father.

I know for some it is difficult to understand that I would choose one such as they are for a Task of Personal Service, One of Divine Plan. The difficulty in them understanding, is because they have not walked the Path of Communication that I Am, but that does not mean they are less in any way.

It is like it is in the world. Certain individuals have certain responsibilities. All could not have the same. It would confuse the issues, but also would not spread the responsibilities.

I know I speak differently, but it is to encourage individuals to see the broad side of seeing all issues, and not just what they would feel is not how they would deal with the conditions, the situations, and/or the reasonabilities that prevail.

I close these Words, but with much Love to all human beings, because to walk the human path is a *Gift* Far Greater than it is seen or known to be.

Service to The Creator is *the step* that one day will help the individual more fully understand how Important it is to learn and to address subjects never before experienced in the human plan."

AUGUST 29, 2005 AT 12:55 P.M.

OUR HEAVENLY FATHER
MANY SAINTS

"I am your Heavenly Father.

There were Others standing Here with Me, because We were discussing a very Important Matter. We All smile at this *little one* who takes each Word and knows the Importance of It.

You live in a time where there are many indiscretions in how individuals should handle their personal communications, and also, how they perceive others to be who, in many ways, there is much conversation between all of them, but oftentimes dismissing the communication as just ordinary, when it is a volume of things that should be discussed for the real meaning that they represent.

I speak differently, but I know you will understand, due to the fact that all human beings speak in a different degree, a different concept on many subjects because, in their determination in wanting to get a point across, they oftentimes dismiss the facts because they are so lengthy.

Throughout the world there are millions of human beings who never think of the importance in what they speak, the value of it, the condition of it, or the method used that others will hear or read, or be caused to participate in, in some form, some manner.

I speak differently today, because it is rare that an individual looks into *a conversation* in the degree that they should. They take so much for granted, and they pass over certain words that could be distressful to them, to their meaning, because the wording is appointed in a manner of discernment that is not perceived in its full degree, or measurement, or evaluation, or consideration.

I know I am speaking in a very difficult way, but when you speak to others, think of what you are saying, think of the repercussions your wording could cause, or the lack of understanding, because in the *Gift of human life* there are *so many Gifts* attached to how you see, how you think, how you look, what you speak, and how you show yourself to others.

I will close, but I have only spoken these Words to alert you to What We Saints Here in the Heavens see occurring consistently, and sometimes it is overlooked to the point where it is not seen for the value of it, or how it can affect your presence with others; in other words, accepting the words spoken."

AUGUST 29, 2005 AT 1:49 P.M.

"There are Many of Us present. (He's smiling.)

Many times when We know *this little one* is available to speak Words that will give to others more understanding and more various abilities to perceive what a Great Gift Divine Love Is, and how We Here in the Heavens accept It as a *privilege*, and We desire to be a Part of It in Association and Communication with those who participate in It.

You live in a time wherein there are so many factors, so many differences in opinions, so many abilities to be right over wrong, pure over impure, just over injustice. You live in a time that will be *a memorable time* because of so much that occurs in the spiritual growth of the human mentalities that are in the living state at this time.

Some may ask Me why I spoke a Statement such as This One was. I can answer that. You live in a time that, in many ways, has closed out other periods of time that were not very assuring about The Divine in Its Right Measure of how It is a very close way to all human beings. It is a means to participate in responding to the Saints, responding to the measures that make one think of a prayer, or of the decision to help someone else spiritually, that for a long time, was not there.

Needless to say, there is so much that this time in the history of human living, human lives, have the opportunity to speak more in an outward manner, awakening the minds of perhaps millions of human beings. At other times the number was selected in the Spiritual Role, not allowing or not encouraging those who live the normal factors in life, who have been endowed with the abilities to stand openly, speak openly, *in wording to stress more fully the Importance of Sainthood and that It is a Goal to be thought about for the Soul that must be returned to It from Where It came.*

Needless to say, hundreds or even thousands of hours could be spent on addressing this Subject Matter, and making use of the time with showing All the Assets of The Divine, encouraging all ages to look for that **Goal**, participate in what is necessary to rise emotionally, physically, spiritually, to one day being a human being known to speak from Heaven, and be termed **'Divine'**."

AUGUST 30, 2005 AT 12:17 P.M.

OUR HEAVENLY FATHER

"We are taking *the little one* to the Foot of The Cross. She stands looking up, shocked by what she sees — the form of a Human Being bearing nails and other things. The Cross bears the heavy weight of not just the body, but all that the body wears and sometimes conceals, *because of the possessiveness that is innate in human intentions and wills.*

There is a degree of speech amongst those standing. She says to them: If The Father Wills you to be part of this, I plead with you to be sure it is beneficial to your good will, but also, to how you think, how you act, how you speak, and how you live with others like yourself, or those who cannot yet practice what you feel you desire and will to be seen with, for, and why it occurs on you, because of you.

I have never held this *little one* this indepthly close to What'I Am, Who I Am. The *closeness* is to give her the strength to continue What I Will others to hear about, to see, and to more fully understand, that in the passages of human life, human living, many things can and will occur that will not be pleasing to the mentality, as you know mentality to be, but you must also be aware of what your attitude, what you are expressing, is in keeping with Divine Will, not just your desire for attention that obviously says is *not Sacred* in any degree, source, or even suggested as what you would love or like human life to be.

So much has been delivered for such a long time. All of the Saints Who spoke and Who speak, want to create in human living, *the innate desire and goal to be all that The Father Wills them to be*, because of the Beauty and Divine Love for the *Soul*.

What I speak at this time, may be inconceivable in concept to those who read It, but some of the things were not what would be practical or pleasant to The Holy Trinity, because of their lack of innate desire for purity, genteelness, respect and honor, to be evident to the point where there can be no misconception to the Words.

Human life has a way of wanting all things to be correct, but never not remember, that when you are associated in a different atmosphere, you have the responsibilities to not fall in what We would call 'a Masonic trap'.

Maybe to some, What was just put into print will be difficult to comprehend how Important It is, to see It for what It is, and to bring your mentality back to

knowing what is improper, unjust, impure, and has no respect for The King to respond to, because What was spoken was, in many ways, to give you Something to think about in a way, a manner and a degree that shows it is Important for you to counsel yourself on what avenue you will take, follow, and *practice only what is Important for the Soul that is the recipient of all you think, speak, accept, follow in every aspect of human living.*

My Words are different, but My Love Far More Divine, because it is My Love that wants all Souls to *withdraw from anything* that is suggestive to the deterioration of sound, not just moral, but conscious understanding of *what the Gift of human life was created for.*

***No human being created is never not a Blessing of The Divine. Remember this all the time.*"**

AUGUST 30, 2005 AT 2:10 P.M.

SAINT CATHERINE OF SIENA

"I am Saint Catherine of Siena.

So Many of Us Saints enjoy this time that We spend in delivering to others Our Understanding and Our Desire to let others know how We act, how We feel, how We observe, and how We practiced the type of living We felt would help Us save Our Soul.

Every human being has the purpose, the reasonability, the logic, and the understanding of so many facts, interests, parts and preferences in the way of living as a human being. Even children reach a point when they adjust to what they feel they are accepted in doing, in their home, and also when they are away from home, in someone else's home, or even in a store that they might be visiting.

Human life was created with the Gift of knowledge, the Gift of perception, the Gift of understanding, and the Gift of what would be acceptable in the eyes of others, and in what others would consider moral or immoral, just or unjust, truth or fiction. The list is endless, due to the fact that a human intellect has many diverse conditions, situations, abilities, choices, and chances.

Now these Words may not sound feasible but, in many ways, they contribute insight into how an individual *should choose* what is moral over what is immoral, what is just over what is unjust, what is regular over what is irregular, what is practical over what is impractical, what is pure over what is a sin.

The Beauty in the Gifts of human living is that there are so many basic facts that give to the mentality what is proper over what is improper, what is feasible over what is infeasible, what is fun over a trick. A trick may be out of context, because it all depends upon what the trick would mean, or would bestow on the meaning if it was associated with another form of action.

As I close these Words, I close Them with much love for human life, because it has so many decisions to act properly, purely and in justice.

Always remember: *When you are in doubt, don't change what you feel is correct. If you are ever in fear, always remember to say some prayers and ask The Father to help you. He will, but also, He might say, 'Make this change in what you are thinking or doing. It will be the answer that you need.'"*

AUGUST 30, 2005 AT 3:03 P.M.

THREE SAINTS

"There are Many of Us present. It is always a delight when We hear that Words will be spoken that are not just ordinary, but Words either of Direction or Commitment, or Words to give Hope in how an individual lives.

There are Three of Us standing together. We are ready to partake in a Great Miracle. The Miracle is at this time, Wording to encourage all ages of human living to understand that the *Gifts* of human way, human life, have a purpose to strengthen certain situations, conditions, and also, to give hope when and where it is needed.

You live in a time wherein so many things are different than they could claim to be many years ago. The changes are to give strength, dignity and purpose *to* and *for* the lives of thousands and thousands of human beings. It is amazing how much strength courage can induce. It is amazing that how much knowledge can encourage a human being to feel secure; also, the ability to participate, the ability to contribute one's knowledge, one's facts, one's interest, and one's courage to stand up for what is not just profitable, but strengthening to one's will and to one's abilities regarding knowledge.

Let Me take now why the Importance of Spiritual Understanding is such a Great Asset to a human being. It is Important for thousands of individuals to understand that the very thought of the Heavenly Ones instills hope, communication, and also, a unification of Will, of Stature, and of the ability and the privilege to be able to speak to Someone Who is titled to be **'a Saint'**.

You live in a time in which so much is changing, so much is becoming more evident to your mentality, and to your ability to participate in things, whether they are just verbal or a participation that is physical, that give interest to the mind and the perception of what could be, that would be more interesting, or that give more to life physically, mentally, morally.

As you say your prayers each day, no matter what time you choose, remember, you are heard, and even though you do not hear a confirmation of what you have just spoken, you have the strength to feel that you were heard, and then the strength to persevere in doing what you feel would be not just practical, but feasible for certain areas in which you live, and you know others who also could use what you decided would be practical to your way of living or give strength to your knowledge, thus giving you abilities to persevere under conditions not usual to you.

The Greatest thing you can learn is that, **One: You should accept that there is 'A Divine Creator' that is always present.**"

AUGUST 31, 2005 AT 11:58 A.M.

MANY SAINTS

"We oftentimes use *one small voice* to reach a numerous number of others, to help them in ways they would not have thought about regarding the *Importance*, the *Privilege*, and many other *Gifts* for human beings, to fulfill the Will of The Creator for a time to come.

We All speak when We are requested to speak, using *one voice* to repeat What The Heavenly Father Wills others to learn about, to stand strong regarding, and also, preparing the Souls of those who take the Words and those who read the Words, to a stronger attitude, perception, even a stronger inclination to follow what the Soul will be happy because of, *the 'Goal' that the Soul has been made aware of, for a later time.*

We All know that Our Words are not exactly as you speak, but They are Words to comfort you, and to give you the strength to follow what is morally sound, pure, just, instead of partaking in what *the enemy* would pass before you that would not give you what you need to have.

We speak differently through *this little one*, because We could not tell you these Things in a manner and way that you would know It to be Direct, in how It can be determined, unless it is done the Way We are doing it this day.

You are loved more than you know. The Love is from The Divine. The Heavenly Father, The Creator of All Things, has given to the world Words to encourage, to instill the desire to return to Him, as 'a Saint'."

AUGUST 31, 2005 AT 12:58 P.M.

OUR HEAVENLY FATHER

"There are Many of Us present because of What We would like to speak regarding *the Creation of human beings.*

Let Us take now what a human being consists of, all the things that make it *a living being*. Let Me take your *heart*, your *lungs*, your *intestinal tract*. Now, let Me take the *veins* that you have within you. They have a purpose also. Now let Me take the *bones* that give support to each section of your physical.

You have the *knowledge* to think of these portions of how you live, plus the other portions of human living that you could not, not want within you.

The human body was designed for many things to be able to be practiced with it. There are countless numbers of things that are not talked about at all, because each portion of human parts in a body say something different, and yet sometimes are a portion of one or more other things, making it valuable to how you live, important to how you live. The nails you have, have a purpose, not always seen as something on your fingers or your toes, but they have a purpose.

Now you, as a human being: The Gift of *speech*; it is of great importance also, because you depend upon it also. All the features of your body —your eyes, your nose, your chin — each portion would be difficult at this time to put into print, because in the Creation of human life, *much was thought about* in giving to human life *the foundation,* for the abilities to use in many ways, without crippling an individual to not be able to be supported in a different facet of living.

The Creation of human life is never really thought about in 'the Greatness and The Divine Love' that had to be 'a Major Portion' of designing it.

Needless to say, hundreds of pages in writing could be written on the detail of every facet in the Design of human life. As some may read This, they might wonder why I would speak in this manner.

I, your Heavenly Father, unless you recognize what *a Tremendous Gift you are the custodian of*, you cannot fully understand what it took, *the Mentality it took,* to design human living in the Degree of so much Importance, so much Practicality, and yes, Feasible, to be able to accept in the daily way of living.

Now, let Us take *'a Portion'* you never see: *That is your 'Soul'. The Soul is a 'Living Companion' to you the moment you are created a human being.* The Soul tolerates many things: how you think in every facet of life. The Soul is the *recipient,* and the Soul is *'That Portion'* that is to be returned to *Me.*

Who is *Me*? Do you have any concept of Who *'Me'* means? Basically, *It is The Creator of All Things.*

I could speak thousands of hours on What I have just delivered verbally.

I ask you to think about this when you pray: Do you remember to say,

> *'I love You, God, thank You for the privilege of my creation, a human being, because through it You have given me the opportunity to return 'that Portion' within it that You Are, and It can be called "A Saint", and it is my understanding, Father, that It will be in a Living State with You, forever and ever and ever.'"*

SEPTEMBER 1, 2005 AT 12:01 P.M.

OUR HEAVENLY FATHER
OUR HEAVENLY MOTHER

"I am your Heavenly Father; and I smile when I say, 'I am your Heavenly Mother.'

We have come together on this day to tell you that We appreciate the way you act, aiding others to understand more indepthly, the Importance of Words being sent through *one small voice*, thus giving to those who read the Words, a greater understanding that We do participate in their way of living, and We do care, more than they know it to be, because you see, We, too, walked the way of humanity; We, too, had responsibilities, personal in every way.

Today as I speak these Words, I did it to give you an understanding of Divine Love that, in many ways, is constantly available to you.

The Father blesses those who ask for a Blessing, and those who, perhaps, deserve a Blessing and do not know that they are being blessed.

As I close these Words, I say, 'Never forget you are loved by The Holy Trinity for how you share your time and life, putting into script and following through on Words that will aid others to more fully comprehend and understand, that *there is a Heaven for you.*'"

SEPTEMBER 1, 2005 AT 2:07 P.M.

OUR HEAVENLY FATHER

"I am your Heavenly Father.

You have heard My next Statement before: *'You do live in a time worse than Sodom and Gomorrah.'* To just speak the Words should let you know that throughout the world so much evil, impurities are being practiced. There are many excuses for this to occur, but excuses are just to justify an impure act. So many individuals, of all degrees of intellect, cater to their emotions, their moods, and/or their weaknesses that are morally infected by the *enemy*.

Some will say, 'Who is the *enemy*?' *Satan* works hard, and he does not avoid one step that will satisfy his manner of doing things that are so vile and contemptible morally, psychologically, physically. The list is endless on the different areas of human life that the evil one will try to enter, abuse, and cause serious immoralities.

These Words, to some individuals, will not mean much, because they do not see themselves being morally weak to the point where it is a sickness, immorally based on what they feel is natural to the human manner of living.

We so often hear the Statement that *'You live in a time worse than Sodom and Gomorrah.'* There are many times in the history of the creation of human lives that there were many ugly, arrogant occurrences that *ignored the Soul* in human beings, human life, human living; thus, casting aside What should be treated with *respect*, and definitely *thanksgiving*, for the chance to live the human way and reach for the time to return to The Creator, and become *'a Saint'*.

Needless to say, hours and hours could be spoken on what is beneficial and what gives to one's way of life, way of living, a manner that encourages the individual to base things on *Purity*, in Honor of The Holy Father, on *Dignity* in an honorable way, and also, never forgetting what a Blessing The Beloved Heavenly Mother is, because of how She was created to be The One that others would have to look to and be able to pray to, and respect Her in an Ultimate Way, because *She represents Purity of the mind and the body and the Soul, but also, of what a Beautiful Way to live as a woman in the world.*

So much could be spoken on this Description of how those in the living state now, and even before this, could have a beautiful life, living it daily, and yet being able to say that everything they did, they thought, they spoke, was purely done and pleasing to Divine Way."

SEPTEMBER 4, 2005 AT 9:40 A.M.

OUR LORD

"You have been gifted to live in a time in which more understanding of The Divine's Presence is more obvious to a greater degree of men, women and children, but I am sad to say, *'It is not understood for What a Gift It is from The Divine.'*

So much, or I could say, too much is taken for granted, thus ignoring what a Precious Gift has openly been spoken about, to enlighten all ages to the *Privilege* they are the recipients of.

So little is spoken about regarding what *a Gift of this Measure* is to those who receive *It, a Gift of Divine Love* which is over human love or human understanding.

When I was nailed to a cross, it had many reasons: anger, jealousy, and words too numerous to mention.

Human understanding is not always what it should be, not because it has not been instructed upon, but because other gifts to humans from human beings, precedes what *This Gift* does mentally, morally, logically, for the physical and, of course, the *Goal* for which human life was created to reach.

Though these Words are different than some would expect Them to be, I have chosen Them because the meaning of Them is understandable to all mentalities.

A Gift of Divine Love is not always appreciated, but I assure you, *Its Purpose is Divine, and gives aid where it is needed, plus an innate understanding that I Exist.*"

SEPTEMBER 4, 2005 AT 12:10 P.M.

MANY SAINTS

"Many of Us are always present where *this little one* is. The responsibilities are humongous in Value, Concept, and Divine History.

We hold *the little one* tightly, because the Power We use for her to be able to repeat Our Words is always beyond what It is expected to be, even by Us Who The Father uses in so many ways, so many times, especially in this Personal Gift of Divine Love, and of course, The Holy Trinity is ever present.

A Blessing of this Degree, Purpose and Logic is beyond what the human mentality can perceive; also, as the Words flow through to her, in her, from her, Many of Us are aware of *the Power a Gift of this Divine Love is, to allow such a Communication to be heard.*

There are millions of men, women and children who should be getting, receiving What is delivered through her, even if they feel It too difficult for them to believe, because they *innately sense* the Power through which the Words flow has to be real.

A Blessing of this Major Divine Love is Obvious because of What It speaks so openly, so clearly, thus encouraging the necessity or the need to think what It means, and how Important It is, to how they accept It morally, psychologically, emotionally, mentally.

We will close these Words at this time, because the Power We used for the Words to be spoken, was difficult for *the little one's* body at this time."

SEPTEMBER 6, 2005 AT 12:05 P.M.

OUR HEAVENLY FATHER

"I am your Heavenly Father.

When I knew it was My Time to go to the earth and walk it amidst all who were in the living state, I knew also, I would be bound by Divine Will to instruct What was necessary for those in the living state at that time, to hear clearly the Lessons that were delivered, because of the Souls that would be the victims of wrong, *if these Lessons were not heard in their Full Measure, Reasoning, Purpose and Divine Love.*

There have been other times in the history of human lives that different individuals were sent to speak, to act, to deliver, to encourage, and to enlighten the purpose *for which human life was such a Gift of Divine Love.*

Again, today in your time, I am doing this through *one small voice, one small body*, and each time I speak, it is to help those, not just the ones present, but wanting What I speak to be put into print for several ages yet to come, to understand *'how close'* I am to them, for them, based on Divine Love, not just human interpretation.

Though I speak often, and perhaps it could be tiring and a burden, *I beseech you to accept It as a Gift of Divine Love for the Souls Who will be given the opportunity to be returned to Where I Am, for All Eternity.*

Children should be instructed in a manner and way understandable to them, so when they pray they will know they are speaking to Someone in a Living State of Love for them.

I could speak endlessly, because it is so Important for human beings of all ages, all backgrounds, all dimensions of personal understanding, *to see the Reality of such a Gift as This One Is,* **because there is nothing else created that would be as Sufficient, as Caring, as My Divine Love for you. Remember this."**

SEPTEMBER 6, 2005 AT 12:58 P.M.

SAINT CATHERINE OF SIENA
SEVERAL SAINTS

"**I** smile when I say, 'I am Saint Catherine of Siena.' There are Several of Us present, due to the fact that when The Father Decreed We would have the privilege to speak Words through this Gift, that would give to others a sound reasonability of understanding *'how close' The Creator and All the Saints are to each of them.*

When you pray, you pray to Someone you cannot see, but your prayer is based on your love for The Heavenly Father, The Heavenly Mother, and Other Saints Here, because logic tells you it is A Supreme Power Far Beyond what your daily life is accustomed to. The Power is a Gift of Communication, for the ability to communicate because of What The Divine stands for.

When you say, 'A Saint is Divine,' you say more than you think you say, because you sense, you understand, and you associate The Heavenly Kingdom with Those Who are appointed There at a given time, and it is logical for you to say, *'They are in the Divine, I can pray to Them and They will answer me, or They will help me in what I am requesting to be, to have, to understand whatever my reasoning is; I know there is Someone in the Heavens that will know how, why I am speaking the way I am.'*

Think about this: If you were created in a different species of living, would it not be sad not to have the communication with All the Saints that are with The Holy King? Would it not be a feeling of despair without that Beautiful Gift of Divine Love that He shares with you, Our Heavenly Mother shares with you, and Those Who have the privilege to be named 'Saints'? They have the privilege to share with you, your privilege of sharing with Them?

Now, What I am going to speak is a little different. Let Us say that you live in the human way and you want someone to please you, to help you, and the practical thing for you to do is to go to them and tell them how you need their help, or their encouragement, or perhaps even a loan of monetary measure. As human lives were given the permission and the realization that as they communicate with each other on small matters, big matters, or health matters, it gives assurance, it gives hope, it gives understanding, and it gives a strength to being a human being with the privileges you are endowed with, and that is belief, that is trust, that is assurance, that is hope.

I know I speak differently, but *to be a human being has so many assets and a Beautiful Goal to one day reach, for your*

Soul to return to The Creator of All Things.

Some might want to say, *'Why would this be delivered in this degree, this manner?'* The Father, in His Love, The Holy Mother, in Her Love, knows what can help you in many ways, many times, and there are Many Saints in the Heavens that have a very similar Gift from The Divine, but never forget, when you were created a human being, there were more *Gifts* available through your lifetime, but the basic things you are assured of is that, ***as you love The Heavenly Father, The Heavenly Mother, and All the Saints that you know to be, you have more than Friends, you have Those Who understand life and are willing to aid you when They feel They can.***"

SEPTEMBER 6, 2005 AT 2:24 P.M.

OUR HEAVENLY MOTHER

"I am your Heavenly Mother.

I have come today to tell you, in a Personal Way, how beautiful it is in what you are doing, how you are doing it, sharing with others so many things that they would never have the privilege to know about. Your discussions are numerous and enjoyable, because you see so much in so many things. You respond. That is not always the case with many people. You have an opinion. It is usually regarding compassion, sincerity, or an interest in what is occurring, giving to your manner of living, informative information that causes you to think, to respond, to participate and to be able to communicate with others.

I, your Heavenly Mother, find it sad when I see so much quiet and few words exchanged when there is a need for it, or a necessity for it, because what speech does, it gives strength to the mental, the physical, and the spiritual association with others.

Granted, I do not say silence is not necessary, but I do say, 'Communication gives something for others to think about, and to judge their emotions or sensitivities or confusions or abilities on the subject matter alone; thus, giving to daily living something other than no speech, no concern, no satisfaction, thus making it boring to the mind and to the way how one works.'

How I have spoken may sound odd, but even Here in the Heavens We communicate, not exactly as you do, but communication gives to the mentality something to use, to keep active with, by, for. It can give pleasure, or something new to think about, or it can even give excuses in many things.

Many might wonder why I would talk like this. I assure you, it is because in the Gift of human life, human living, *speech* was an active Subject, Gift, because *through speech there is communication*, but also, *the human mentality* is another *Gift*. It adds to many portions of human living that gives merit, gives hope, and allows an individual to partake in what could be feasible, or reassuring, or comfortable.

I, your Heavenly Mother, could speak hours on this Subject, because it is a Subject that gives to the mentality, gives to the physical what many times is needed, keeping the mental active and keeping the physical active, especially when it is natural to use and enjoying to hear, and gives subject matter, something to think about.

One of the reasons for *prayer* was to encourage human beings of all ages to use prayer to keep them occupied, and able to more fully understand more than they would if there was no such thing as prayer. Prayer can be comforting, it can be enjoyable, it can be soothing, it can give hope. These are but a few of the beautiful assets of the word *'prayer'*.

Human life is gifted with many things: good, practical, enjoyable and happy are the main points. The points that others may find good for them could be their moods, indifferences; the list is endless, but where there is happiness, there is progress, hope, enjoyment and a deeper understanding of the *Gifts* of human life that have so much, aiding human life in many ways, purposes and goals.

Always remember, God loves you, and He designed all things for every human being to be able to use what they thought, or they could do, or they could feel, not pain, but interests, giving to them that *they were human, and were given the role to live it and be happy as a human, based on God's Love for allowing you to be created a human being.*"

SEPTEMBER 7, 2005 AT 11:10 A.M.

OUR HEAVENLY FATHER

"Even though it does not appear so, We are always present where *this little one* is. The Magnitude of Responsibilities she is forced to undergo is a Miracle unto itself, because most is never shown. To walk the path that she walks, it is a lonely road, even when there are hundreds or even thousands of human beings in the sight, as though they are all close to her.

You live in a time wherein so much looks natural to many walks of life, living the human way. In one way this is a Gift of Divine Love, because in so many ways it stresses purity of the mind, generosity of the will, and hope in the spiritual for the Souls Who come in contact with What is called '*Revelations*'; thus, in many ways, instructing gently '*how close*' the Heavenly Ones are at all times, not just when someone is praying.

It is important for all ages to be aware of how Divine Love is shared to all human beings. The greatest one is the birth, and then comes the time when they are made aware of The Divine, Who created them, and facts such as these are, to give them the strength, the understanding, and the Purpose for What they were created to attain, and to one day return to The Creator and be called *'a Saint'* by Him.

So much is so beautiful and a treasure to be a part of. Animals, trees, and many other living things do not have this background, this Goal, this Future, but they do have a temporary time for those in the living state to use them for many things, thus being thankful for them in a human manner of thinking.

My Words are unusual, but They are spoken to strengthen one's understanding of *what a privilege it is to be born a human being*, encircled by all the Gifts that give to human living, human life, so many Gifts that give hope, amusement, and also protection. I must add another one: the food you eat supports your system, your physical. It is a Gift of Divine Love you may never think of, but it was designed to give you what you would need. It is important, because it gives you strength. It serves the body well, to be able to live in the manner and way it was created to be.

I could speak hours on this subject; perhaps I will at another time, but as I close these Words today, always remember: To be created in the human way of living is a *Blessing far greater* than it is seen to be, because it says, '*I, your God, love you.*' Never forget What I have just said."

SEPTEMBER 7, 2005 AT 11:55 A.M.

THE HOLY TRINITY

"The first time I asked The Heavenly One if I could print What I felt He spoke, He said to Me, 'Yes, Son, I am sure You will do it in Honor of Who I Am, and for the good of Souls.'

So much could be spoken on the Importance of words, because what they contain has meaning, purpose, reasonability, and oftentimes depicts a very important subject that could give hope to an individual, or more than one human being, because the *Gift of speech* was designed to be able to speak words in a continuous form, manner, way, for a purpose to be understood for more than one word would say, but also, the communication through the voice is of the greatest importance, because the *sound* puts strength in what is spoken, and many times does more than if the words were just put into words.

I hold *the little one* tightly, because I use her so many times for things I would like to speak to everyone individually, but that would be an impossibility because of the number of human lives that would be available, if it were one at a time.

I love those who accept *What I have given through one small voice*, because in the Words, there is a Message Beyond what the Words with Sound would have been able, enable, unable, to penetrate for a given, lengthy time.

I speak so differently each time I speak through *this little one*, because there is so much to be spoken, due to how I feel about human lives.

I will close My Words at this time, but I promise you, each time I speak, even if you cannot hear Me, I bless you from The Divine."

SEPTEMBER 7, 2005 AT 2:17 P.M.

SAINT CATHERINE OF SIENA

"There are Many of Us present. I am Saint Catherine of Siena.

Whenever We hear happy discussions or memories on what occurred when Some of Us Saints were present on what was going on at the time, it is always a joy to hear that We were recognized as being present.

So many times when The Heavenly Father requests One of Us to speak, or to be present, or encourages Us to partake for the good that could occur or will occur if We are present, it is a happiness beyond what words can say, describe.

Today has been a lovely day, because Many of Us are present. We hear you speak and We are not just listening out of curiosity, but *This Gift The Father has given to the world is a Blessing for All of Us, because It shares with others the beautiful understanding regarding being a human being, and one day, hopefully, going to Heaven.*

Children of all ages should understand that *to live in the human way is God's Plan.* It is not always spoken regarding this fact, but some just say 'The Heavenly Mother'. We smile at this, because it pleases Her when She knows that a child will be created and loved abundantly.

As you walk in the manner you walk for the purpose that you expound on writing What is spoken to give you more Information on The Divine's Intercession on all you think, say and do, The Father loves this Miracle, because He created It for a Reason, a Purpose, Personal in many ways, but a Beauty in how individuals can compare notes, and can compare what they feel is necessary to return to The Creator and be called 'a Saint'.

So much has been delivered just to encourage those who take the Words and those who will read Them, to always remember **there had to be A Creator of All Things.** How else could all be where it is? There would be no way for it to just happen, because in the Creation of all things, and in the Creation of human living, human lives, **there had to be One Greater, to be able to design everything in the Beauty it is and always was.**

You are loved for all you do, and never forget, when you speak, you are heard, and when you laugh, you are heard, and when you wish, you are heard, and when you pray, Many Here in the Heavens hear your way. **Never forget, God loves you too."**

SEPTEMBER 8, 2005 AT 12:43 P.M.

OUR HEAVENLY MOTHER

"I am your Heavenly Mother.

We All smile as *the little one* recognizes how Many are Here with Me. We have come at this time to hopefully assist you in the tasks you have accepted for The Divine. I say it this way to assure you that when you walk aiding, helping, and in many ways encouraging other individuals to follow a path you know to be not just delegated, not just designated, but practiced, to follow the Will of The Creator because of Souls.

When you buy something and you like something, you enjoy it, you love it, you do not want anything to happen to it, do you? It is a treasure, and you enjoy having it. When you are created a human being, you are instilled, gifted with the Greatest Gift you could ever receive. *That is your 'Soul'.*

Your physical abilities are so important, and it is always something to see when We see someone checking out what they are capable of using with their hands, their feet, their arms, their neck, their face, because these attributes have reasons, purposes, and in many ways it is sad to be without one of them, let alone several of them.

The reason I am speaking this way is to make you aware that human life was created with so many *Gifts*, giving to it what others things did not have: first of all, the mind. The mind has the ability to do many, many things. Even a baby, when it is hungry, will cry. It does not know why, but it responds.

Human life was created a beautiful way, with so many attributes and so much reasoning for everything it possesses, and everything it uses to grow to adulthood at a given time.

Why do I speak this way today? It is important to be reminded that you are not a stick in the ground, you are not a piece of paper that others control. You have abilities mentally, physically; the list is endless.

I come to you today, not just to remind you, but to alert you to *what a Gift human living, human life has*, because it has a *Future* to it, a *Goal* for it, and it should be innate in you to look for what you must practice, partake in, accomplish, to reach that *Goal* for the *'Portion' of you that is 'a Portion' of The Creator*, even the whole time It is within you.

A Gift of Divine Love was given to human life, showing the Importance of being created a human being. *Love from The Father is Greater than It is seen to be. Never forget this."*

SEPTEMBER 8, 2005 AT 1:45 P.M.

SAINT JOSEPH, THE HOLY SPIRIT

"I am Saint Joseph.

I come on this day in appreciation for how you respond to All the Saints. It is Important that All you have been able to gather, to give to others more Personal Informative Understanding of *Sainthood as a Goal for their Soul,* to one day be in Heaven with The Creator.

I know I speak differently, but I speak today because I am fully aware how much you care about Us Saints. Oftentimes, We hear requests and We know that the individual or individuals are desiring for Us to aid them, to encourage them, to help them in some form, some way, some degree. We do all We can to help what is necessary, what is needed; you can be sure of that.

I speak today because of so much personal attention and love that We receive through *this Gift* that you work in, work for, regarding the Importance of Sainthood. It is indeed a pleasure to hear all you speak and how you help others more indepthly understand to be aware of The Divine Measure of Divine Love, Divine Hope for the Souls that appreciate all you think, say and do.

So much could be spoken at this time in honor of those who have the Faith to secure the ability of others to be able to stand strong, and use The Divine for many ways, many reasons, many purposes, many goals.

Needless to say, God loves you for your effort to help others know, that to communicate with The Divine is always seen in a loving manner, way, and you can be assured that you are heard, you are never forgotten, and you are, in many ways, helped in degrees that you may not understand, but it is always available in how you think and how you plan and how you live, according to Divine Love, in your manner and way."

SEPTEMBER 9, 2005 AT 12:06 P.M.

OUR HEAVENLY FATHER

"I am your Heavenly Father.

There are so many times I would like to speak to all of you at one time, because I have so much to give you Information on that, ordinarily, you would not have access to. One of these things is of Great Importance: First, no human being is aware of *how close* Many Saints are to them every moment of every day; but needless to say, I, your Heavenly Father, know everything you think, do and say, because I created you to one day return a *Portion* of you to be with Me forever and ever and ever.

I speak through *one small voice*. I always smile when she hesitates as I speak My Words. She says, 'Be sure, Father, It is You,' and I repeat to her, 'I would not have it any other way.'

I have also come today to remind you that in the Creation of human lives, I implanted many, many *Gifts* to assist you in how to live physically, mentally, emotionally. The list is endless, because, do not forget, along with the *Gifts*, I gave you *a conscience* to make you aware of how you would respond in different ways that would be pure, not impure; just, not unjust.

My Words could go on and on and on. In this Creation of Mine, I instilled so many things to give each one a time of happiness, joy, accomplishment and hope, based on My Love for them.

I love you and I cross you with My Hand, and I say, *'Never forget to draw My Attention, because you do when you make The Sign of The Cross.'* It says to Me: *'I know You are present, Holy One. Thank You. Please never leave me.'"*

SEPTEMBER 9, 2005 AT 1:13 P.M.

SEVERAL SAINTS

"There are Several of Us present. We All enjoy speaking to and through *this little one*, because she responds to Us immediately. She says, 'Do All the Saints speak?' and We smile at this, because she is so matter-of-fact when she questions anything.

Ordinarily, no one can hear What We speak to Each Other, but sometimes when We are close to *one* such as she, We will make it a point for Our Presence to be aware of, in certain different ways, of course; not always the same way, because, do not forget, when We speak, you may hear Our Way, Our Voice, not in the manner you are used to hearing sound, but sometimes We are able to speak in what would be called *'Silence'* in the Name of The Holy Father.

Today, as *this little one* sits with you, many things always occur. Many of Us Saints continuously are around her, because of the Importance of the Tasks she has been appointed for, to, with.

The ***world*** is a Gift of Divine Love. To be created ***a Saint*** is a Gift of Divine Love. All the things about being a human being are ***Gifts,*** not always recognized as such, but definitely are ***Gifts*** to give to human living, human associations, human progress. **The**

Gift of knowledge, of understanding, of hope, of imagination, and of Divine Love, give to human life activities, interests, hope, and yes, a drive to succeed in some way, maybe just as a human being.

We All smile as *this little one* speaks to you with Words that might surprise some of you with all the subject matter We have put forth in It.

To be blessed as a human being is *'a Gift' far greater* than it is seen or accepted, because **in the human state of living, you have been promised a Goal for 'that Portion' of you that is 'a Portion of The One Who created you'.**

There are Several of Us here and We All smile at What We have just spoken openly, because to share What We know, and to share What We think and want you to recognize, is definitely **a Gift of Divine Love** that gives to Us a happiness untold."

SEPTEMBER 10, 2005 AT 9:50 A.M.

GOD THE FATHER

"We sometimes help *the little one's* physical endure what she is confronted with, regarding issues that others want her to fail in or to not see in the manner they decree them to be.

I speak these Words to enlighten those with her to help them more fully understand, although *a Gift of Divine Love is evident*, there are numerous human beings who resist, reject, question, and omit such an occasion such as This, to be feasible in their time in which they live, such a time as they live.

Words such as These are given to help those close to *one* such as she, to aid them in understanding, to walk as she walks, to speak as she speaks, logically, is offered by The Holy Trinity, not her will, but her acceptance of obedience to Divine Will."

SEPTEMBER 10, 2005 AT 10:17 A.M.

GOD THE FATHER
SEVERAL SAINTS

"There are Several of Us present. There is so much yet to be accomplished for the sake of Souls to more fully and readily be able to reach the Goal they were created to have.

There are Several of Us present at this time, because of the Importance of the *'Gift' from The Divine, of The Divine*, that is to give Hope, Direction, and instill Understanding that otherwise would not be obviously attained through one's own ability to understand the Importance of Divine Love for the Creation of man.

We use *a small voice*, but *an obedient voice*, because of the Importance of why *'This Gift'* was given: for the benefit of Souls of possibly thousands and thousands of individual human beings who, without understanding, they would have accepted what others felt were valuable statements to aid them, but they were not what they should have been.

So much is taken for granted, on an individual feeling that they have the answers to so many things beyond what others have. *This little one* We use, fears ever making a mistake, but We try to console her because of her love for The Divine and Our Love for her.

A *Gift*, when it is given, usually bears much responsibility, not all understood, but *obvious in some form, manner.*

So much has been delivered in a Loving Way, a Sharing Way, a Generous Way, put into script, being able to be read, or at times when an individual feels the need to want to more readily understand that human life was created for Divine Plan.

I will close, but as I do, I thank you for all your participation, and *the little one* thanks you for being there when she needs you. I smile at this. We All smile at this. It is natural for her to do."

SEPTEMBER 10, 2005 AT 11:27 A.M.

OUR HEAVENLY FATHER

"I am your Heavenly Father.

I come with much happiness because of how I hear you talk, regarding What you have accepted as My Love for human life, and I add, *the little one's* love for Me.

I bless you, and I say, 'Thank you for your time, in service to aid other human beings to more fully understand *how close I am to you and to them.*'"

* * *

2:20 P.M.

"The Soul is The Distributor of all the attributes God gave us."

SEPTEMBER 11, 2005 AT 11:06 A.M.

GOD THE FATHER

"Son, I am so pleased with your consideration, because of My Love in how I use *a Small Gift*, reminding those who reveal It, in My Existence and My Caring for them as an individual Soul, body and life, and a manner of living in how I created them.

Service in honoring My Will is pleased by Me more than it is understood to be. Granted, I am happy when an individual speaks words to Me, formal and/or informal, but when I am allowed to give to someone *a 'Gift' that depicts My True Presence, I am so happy to be Part of this Union in which I am The Deliverer, in a Personal Way, of My True Existence to the body and to the Soul.*

I speak differently, but it gives Me happiness to reveal My Personal Feeling to one yet in the living state, and using their Soul as a recipient of Hope, of Communication and Personal Love from Who I Am.

I smile when I say My next Words: *My Love for human life is Greater than It is seen or known to be. I am The Father, and each one who receives Me, I bless in more ways than can be seen.*"

SEPTEMBER 12, 2005 AT 10:50 A.M.

OUR HEAVENLY MOTHER

"I am your Heavenly Mother.

We All smile at *this little one* We speak many Words through.

There are so many things that others should understand more indepthly about, but they are Subjects not ordinary to the average manner of speech in the company of others. For instance, if you were at a social gathering, would you be obvious if you wanted to say a prayer to The Heavenly Mother? Would you openly say in a voice to be heard: *'Hail Mary, full of Grace, The Lord is with Thee'?* Would not the others present respond in a variety of sensitivities regarding a prayer at a time they would not expect it to be?

I say these things to help you to understand that prayer is an important part of human life, human living, and yet, there are many places or times it would not be practical. Is that not so?

I smile at these Words, because They are just to make you feel that you have *the privilege, the honor*, and *The Divine Love* to hear those prayers when you are alone. Loneliness is not always *absolute loneliness*, because within you,

you are the custodian with a Soul. The Soul is never away from you. It is *'a Gift' of Divine Love* that you have to support you many times, but also, to encourage you on what you should act like, or practice that is morally sound, correct, and pleasing to *Who is with you, and you with Him.*

Some individuals reading This may be a little shocked at this Statement, but never forget: *You have the freedom to say prayers and to communicate with The Heavenly Father or any Saint you choose. It is That Precious Communication you are never without, because They all love you, and The Heavenly Father has made things to be like this so no human being is ever alone without Him."*

SEPTEMBER 12, 2005 AT 12:08 P.M.

OUR HEAVENLY FATHER

"I am your Heavenly Father.

I am most happy to be with you because of your trust in Me, your love for Me, and how you seek to help others more fully understand *My Presence is Important to them.*

As you awaken each day, it is a new day in your life, a day to practice many acts, some essential, and some just because they give you happiness. I, your Heavenly Father, know how this is to be, because I, too, walk a path similar to how you walk a path. I always look for what is, what will be *happiness for Me to see*, because *in each human life there is 'a Portion' of Who I Am, What I Am,* and I feel the necessity for It to be a happiness in your manner of living, and what you will to have, to use, to practice, to follow, and to commit to.

Each time I speak to you, this special group that I look forward to, I want you to know that I truly love you, because it is innate in you to want to spread What I Will others to know, to understand, to follow, for the sake of their Soul.

When I say My next Word, I smile; the Word is *'Amen'*."

SEPTEMBER 12, 2005 AT 12:32 P.M.

GOD THE FATHER

"In fulfilling a Gift of human living called *'human life'*, there were many decisions that had to be clarified and established so they would be not just practical, but beneficial to the *Soul* of a human being, because *the Soul would be 'That Portion'* of it that would be returned to The Creator, of Who I Am, What I Am, thus being aware of the Importance that would be necessary for what was Pre-planned for the Soul: to produce, to protect and to supply the Soul which They would be in for the benefits that eventually, one day, would be in *The Realm of Holy Atmosphere* and be *'a Saint'*, not just in name, but in duties, in performance, and in acceptance of this responsibility, because of its tremendous need to not just supply the name or the existence of Who they represented, but to benefit It in a Future Manner of Life, of Living, of Association with The Divine.

I could speak hours on this, but it is of such Great Importance, that *the little one* I use must have a short rest between What More is to be delivered regarding this Subject Matter that is a Treasure in many ways; that without It being seen for what It was created for, many Souls would be neglected, on how They were to represent the one in whom They were placed at the moment of conception."

SEPTEMBER 12, 2005 AT 1:46 P.M.

"There are always Many of Us present where this *little one* is, because of the Importance of All that is delivered through her many times, and it is Important that More is put into print for others to read, because of how the Words are given by the Saints Here in Heaven, always addressing a Subject Matter that would not only be interesting, but beneficial to their way of life, or to certain circumstances that only They can guide someone on, or help with the purpose in a manner and degree, making it easier to be able to come to a decision regarding the matter and what it means.

You live in a very precious time. I say *'precious'* because of the Sensitivity that is so outwardly expressed and so intimately responded to, on many subjects and for many purposes, not always recognized, but evident in its mere necessity.

Though I speak differently from Another Realm away from where you are, it is The Father's Permission that We can associate in a degree and way with you, to offer you a Subject Matter that you will respond to automatically, and We will receive the response and use it when We know it is what is needed.

We know that Our speaking to you through the Written Words does not make Our Association what It would be nicer to be; but, nevertheless, when you speak to the Saints and you have a discussion to be concerned about, it is sometimes possible that you receive an answer applicable for the means.

Our Heavenly Father loves those who are willing to share What is helpful to aid certain conditions, benefits and needs. *Your prayers are welcomed abundantly, and many times your kind acts close the situation and can be termed 'a Blessing'.*"

SEPTEMBER 12, 2005 AT 2:19 P.M.

OUR HEAVENLY FATHER
SAINT ALPHONSUS LIGUORI

"I am Saint Alphonsus Liguori.

There are Many of Us present wherever you gather, because it is a Blessing for Us to see so much interest, sincere concern regarding the Importance of What you read, What you help others read, what you practice, also what others practice.

Throughout the world, there are so many changes in individuals' manner of how they see cleanliness, and it is not clean, because it is based on impurities of the mind and the body, thus giving to their Soul what would be called *'black'* or *'evil'*.

Prayer is prevalent in many ways, because there is so much concern over what *prayer* really means, and to what degree it should be practiced personally.

Then, there is the Subject of *family*. The family is not seen at times when there should be more consideration, because of the Importance of *morality*. Moral issues do not stop when there is a family, in its manner of practicing what a family life should be like.

You live in a time where so little is understood regarding what is moral over what is immoral, what is just over what is unjust. The list, I promise you, is endless on issues that would surprise most people.

Sin is not thought about in the same degree it used to be. Sins of the flesh are prevalent. The list is endless, because so many individuals do not *sense* or *apply* what is morally sound to their Soul. The Soul is just an *'Entity of Being'* within them. *They do not consider the Soul is the recipient of all the morality and immorality that they practice.*

The list is endless on this Subject, and there are so few individuals willing or able or capable of being able to put into script for others to read, how each one of these things, and even more such as they are, to not just *be screened* but *to be defined*, due to the fact that *the Soul is the recipient of everything an individual thinks, speaks and does.*

Some who will read these Words will cast Them aside, basing their opinions on humanism.

I, your Heavenly Father, say: *Look at what each one means, and what it does to your Soul, and what makes you feel like you do. Are you free, or are you bound to The Will of The Creator of All Things?"*

SEPTEMBER 12, 2005 AT 2:50 P.M.

"There are always Many of Us present wherever *this little one* is. Even though she respects Us and considers Our Time with her of Great Importance, it is difficult for her at times, because she is always concerned in what Impression We are going to leave with others she is surrounded with.

We smile at what she just had Us do. She was concerned that We were going to use the wrong Word, favoring her, so We used the word 'with', thus not announcing Who were surrounding her.

The world is a very busy place. At this moment, if you were to be certain places, you might be shocked by what was occurring. Then, there are other places, if you were present, that would be what would be termed *'Spiritual places'*. Then there would be places where people could be arguing over their own problems, indifferences, and these things would bring out of them a different mood; perhaps, a different nature and personality.

The reason We All speak on these Subjects is because there are so many differences of opinions, differences of likes and dislikes, differences in morality, differences in desires in who to be with, differences in subject matter, unbelievable in different categories of subject matter.

Sometimes We hear individuals when they are about to pray. They make a definite issue of: 'Be sure, God, It's You,' or 'Be sure, So and So, It's You that will hear me.' What I have just delivered sounds very uncouth, unreasonable, doesn't it? It does to Me.

You live in a time that, in reality, was termed *'worse than Sodom and Gomorrah'*. The list would be endless on this, because so many times since the beginning of Creation, were years of learning, years of acceptance, years of rejection, and yet, years of applying what was interesting to one's way of life. Too many words would have to be spoken to signify all the different means that were available through time.

It is Important that when an individual bases his or her Faith on The Creator, The Ultimate Creator, The Holy One, then all things should be pointed to *what would be feasible to please that method of living in the human way. Be consistent, be sincere, and above all things, be faithful*, and always remember that when you choose a special item that you feel is good for your mentality, your Soul, your way of life and for your final Goal, stick with it, and place it in the Hands of The Creator. You can't miss.

I give My Love with these Words, because, you see, I too walked the human path and had to learn what was best for Me."

SEPTEMBER 13, 2005 AT 12:07 P.M.

GOD THE FATHER

"If I were to walk into this room with you, you would expect to see Me as a Man, dressed differently and drawing attention. Is that not so?

Through *'This Gift' of Divine Love*, so much has been delivered through *one small voice*, requesting to put into print What I Will others to know, to understand, to realize, *'how close'* I am to them, and they are to Me, when We can communicate verbally and It be put into print for time to come, to be able to read the Words and remember What was spoken, the Meaning of What was spoken, and the Reality that It was put into print.

Through *'This Gift' of Divine Love*, so much has been instructed, taught, instilled, and given as a Personal Communication with The Divine.

Today as I speak, it is to awaken the minds of those present, but also those who read the Words, that in The Divine Love for human lives, We Care So Deep, So Much, and We, in Our Way, are always available to any request of help, hope, or interest. Granted, you do not hear a return of Sound, but your mentality, in belief in *'how close'* We are to you, you are to Us, is realistic in Logic, Manner, and Divine Love.

I smile through *this little one*, because she does not know What I am about to speak *until* I speak the Words through her, *to be understood as a Personal Communication of Divine Love for human lives.*"

SEPTEMBER 13, 2005 AT 12:51 P.M.

OUR HEAVENLY MOTHER
SEVERAL SAINTS

"I am your Heavenly Mother.

There are Several female Saints Here with Me at this time. We have come to help you understand that What you have chosen to partake in, is of Divine Plan. Because of so much wrong intercession throughout the world, We find it Important for certain female human beings to be example in how they think, how they speak, how they act, and how they, in their way, accommodate others who need to know certain facts on issues that are not always made available to the world.

Never forget, The Mother of The Son of The Father was a *Girl*. When I say the word, *'Girl'*, I do it with respect, love, genteelness, and an inner excitement of seeing how Important Her Mission upon the earth was. It was to pay Honor to Those with Whom She was associated, and then, when She was alone, Her Dignity and Her Manner of addressing subjects of all different backgrounds, gave to Her a remembrance by thousands of those who met with Her at that time: Her Personality, Her Nature, and Her Love for what was pure, truth, logical understanding, and a subject that gave strength, hope, and an In-depth Belief in The Divine.

Needless to say, there are so many things Our Heavenly Mother was the Leader of, not just the custodian, and there were many times that Her Genteelness and Her Love for human lives, gave strength, purpose, hope and history, for the coming of other Souls that needed to know *the Values and the Necessities of being a woman.*

There are so many things I would like to talk about with you on this day, and other days also, because as you stand in the world representing many different facets, portions, areas — the list is endless — of how the female species should look to others, even their own kind.

I smile when I say My next Words: Never forget, I, your Heavenly Mother, love you more than you know, and I am proud to be a Woman, and I am proud to know all of you. Even though We do not face Each Other, there is always that Communication that I enjoy hearing from you, or about you, or with you.

As The Father loves you, I, too, love you, because, do not forget, I, too, am a Female in the world. Many still pray to

Me. I am so pleased with that. It is a Gift of Divine Love to be remembered as The Heavenly Mother once was."

SEPTEMBER 13, 2005 AT 2:19 P.M.

GOD THE FATHER
SEVERAL SAINTS

"There are Several of Us present. We have made it a point to ask to speak to you where you are, because of how conditions, situations in the living different groups of lives, oftentimes openly diminishes the Importance of this time in life, and many excuses, interferences, objectives and personal opinions cause much consternation in coming to a decision applicable, personal, and based on good nature and sincere caring for other human beings.

We hear so many individuals make a common remark: *'You live in a time worse than Sodom and Gomorrah.'* Then, should it not be thought about, and put into detail regarding some other means, some area of innate respect for those who live, and encourage them to look at a different motive, style, or situation and condition that are feasible to what would be comfortable and afford easy access to, because, after all, in being created a human being, *one has the right to live someplace and be happy.*

The world was created by The Creator of All Things. Those who have put rules into practice should be scrutinized in an indelible way, because of the nature of the subject that could be detrimental if it is not seen for the worth it was designed to be.

Ask yourself: Human control should be based on human logic, based on security and social application to what is logical, *without* egotism, arrogance and self-assurance on the part of those who stand just to be important in the eyes of man.

I could speak hours, but it is time, sometimes, for those interested in, or necessary for important changes in how they live, due to the fact that to protect one's self, there must be conditions satisfactory to the necessities for what is needed that is not necessarily professional, but based on human identification according to how one would expect Me, as The Creator, to plan.

Though I speak differently, I sincerely feel I have made it clear that egotism, self-righteousness, arrogance and things of all radical interpretations *should be cast aside,* and only the *dignity of human life* considered for the end results to be what would be honorable

and in good taste, due to the fact that *every human being is blessed with 'a Portion' of The Creator, called 'the Soul'.*"

SEPTEMBER 14, 2005 AT 11:17 A.M.

OUR HEAVENLY FATHER

"I have given to *this little one* a Task of More Importance than even she realizes.

My Will, My Love, My Hope and My Desire for every human being created is to return to Me in Honor and Glory, and be called *'a Saint'*. The word *'Saint'* is not always thought about in the full measure of Content It represents.

The sky is a place designed, not just to enjoy, but it has a purpose. The sun and the moon each have a purpose. When rain falls, it is designed for a purpose. Each thing that an individual was created with, all have a purpose. Fire has a purpose. Rain has a purpose. The air has a purpose. *There is nothing created that does not speak importance for some logical reason that it was created to be known about.*

Granted, some things would not be favorable to the minds because of what they represent, but there have been times that when something was acknowledged in a manner and way different than the sun, the moon, and the stars.

I, your Heavenly Father, will not discuss all the issues, reasonabilities on every item, every fact of what has been created, or designed for a future to be seen, used.

At this time I speak differently, but I speak because of My Love for the Creation of *human life that has the Greatest Goal, and that is to return to Me 'a Portion' of it, the Soul.*

I could speak hours, but I have said at this time What I Willed to be seen, perhaps not fully understood, but there is a Reason of Mine to speak the Words as an Act of Divine Love for the purpose of human life that is associated with Mine."

SEPTEMBER 14, 2005 AT 12:23 P.M.

OUR HEAVENLY FATHER

"I am your Heavenly Father.

The little one is more with Me than with you, because it is of Great Importance that What I have asked her to do, she knows must be accomplished according to My Will, and she pleads with Me to not allow her to make a mistake of any degree.

We All smile at this, because the *Gift of human life* is a *Gift* above and beyond what it is seen to be, what it is recognized to be, what it is used to be. This *Gift* was created to live for a Higher Goal, a Higher Station of Life for the *Soul* that each human being is gifted with at the moment of conception; whether they are male or female, rich or poor, the body, the Soul is of Divine Will. No Greater Gift can anything created be the custodian of.

I could speak hours, because All of Us Here in the Heavens love *This Communication* that is openly seen, shown, through *a Gift of This Measure*, helping even those who have no Faith in The Divine, to stop and think and see the beauty of becoming '*a human source, force of being*' in the world where there are millions of this kind of creations by Divine Love; thus, encouraging each one to understand that within them they have *'a Portion' of Who I Am*, and *'That'* will be the remaining *Factor*, *Gift* at one time when nothing else exists in the living state.

I close these Words with a Blessing, because through What you partake in, it is a stepping stone beyond what you understand It to be. It is a *Gift* of knowing, of seeing, that at some time there is a Beautiful Goal to reach, and that is to return to from Where It came, through years past."

SEPTEMBER 14, 2005 AT 12:59 P.M.

MANY SAINTS

"There are Many of Us present, and I must add to this, many times, because *'This Gift of Divine Love'* deserves all the attention It can receive, due to the fact that It speaks so Importantly and yet Lovingly, to aid all who read the Words to better understand, more fully comprehend, that life in the human way has many *Great Gifts* to it: First of all, its creation; but, as the creation develops, there are facets of beautiful assets that accompany each other, able to describe many things, respond to many things, to deliver many things, and to address Important Words that give strength to the listeners, hope and a direct understanding of *The Existence of This Creator that has the Power to do All Things*, and with this Power, still wants human beings to arrive at many *Talents*, many *Gifts,* so that their manner of living, their way of life, human, is not stripped of being able *to think higher and to be more grateful for the Goal that awaits the Soul of the individuals.*

I could speak hours on *'This Gift'*, because *It is a Gift of Divine Love, awaking the human mind to a Goal to reach that is Higher than It is seen or known to be.* Just as in the human way, each human being likes to have something that is important, and they do many things to reach this goal in many facets of how they live, how they think, but **the Final Gift is One.** It should be thought about and never set aside, because **It is a Gift to return to The Divine forever and ever and ever, bearing God's Love, in thanksgiving for this Privilege.**"

SEPTEMBER 15, 2005 AT 12:02 P.M.

GOD THE FATHER

"I have requested to be able to take this time to speak with you on subjects that perhaps are not ordinarily the focus of conversation.

You live in a time of much moral and immoral confusion based on the *Commandments* that logically speak openly on facets of logical understanding in what *They* want others to see as having a Purpose to follow. Because of what these *Commandments* are capable of leaving in some memories, the opposite of what *They* were addressed to be, I see so many things that are of important matters, conditions, persuasion, consideration and justice that are being *ignored*, with *substitutions* of what comes to being useful, thus *neglecting what They are all about:* for the *protection* of the mental, the moral, plus the social and physical aspects of human living.

I may speak in a different manner on this day, but We, in *Our Close Association*, have become more apt to speak in a Greater Dissension, Perception, Conception of Logic, because it helps in so many ways, to be able to handle more spiritually correct and bound to The Creator's Will for this Creation of human mentalities that has been blessed with an in-depth identification that is easily understandable, and gives to What is spoken more logic, more feasibility, more practicality, and more pleasing to Me.

I will close My Words, because I could speak hours on end, due to My Love for human lives and how much I want them to understand, that though they live in a world of confusion and some illegitimate acceptance, I want them to not only be leaders of What is Spiritually My Will for them, but in their manner of living that others see them for, hear them for, they will leave an impression that will give moral strength, moral obedience, and moral communication where it belongs.

Needless to say, I could speak endlessly, because in My Love for this Creation that I have instilled so much understanding and instruction and applicability to follow, I want all things to be understood *as* and *so* they will give *example* to millions of other human beings."

SEPTEMBER 15, 2005 AT 12:53 P.M.

SEVERAL SAINTS

"Though We are not going to mention certain names because of other things We must or will speak about — those who are ill, the ones you know — granted, it is always a sadness, but you can be assured, The Father is well aware of all situations, combinations and things that occur; but now, I will speak on another Subject. There are Several of Us here.

Each day of life has a purpose and a goal. The ambition of the mentality is often based on what the individual feels he or she wants to develop within them to a degree and manner *exceptional*, whether it be to be known, or for financial reasons. There is nothing wrong with this prayer. It is natural, and for the most part, it is sincere.

The list is endless on what individuals use prayer for. It is a *Wonderful Gift* when it is done with sincerity, hope, understanding and an innate desire for progress or hope to be the aspired will, even of the poorest ones who ask for things to occur.

I speak slowly through *this little one*, because there are so many things she confronts Us with, and We smile at this, because her communication is to accomplish help, aid, hope, or to correct despair, correct illness, and correct an unfairness and make it opposite of what it is doing to certain individuals.

Prayer is meant for every facet of human life, not just a few, because you see, The Holy Father, The Giver of Life, is always present and available to hear.

The Beautiful Part of Prayer is for the good things it requests and the hope that it expresses where hope is the goal and the main factor. The list is so endless and so beautiful. That is why it is so interesting for All of Us Here in the Heavens, when We hear requests for prayers on so many subjects, for so many reasons, thus letting Us participate in their ability, their knowledge, their hope, their love for all the means that could accomplish what is good, what is beneficial, what is logical, what is superior.

The *human mind* is a Gift of Divine Love, and the *human sensitivity*, a Gift of Divine Love, and the *human will* to reach for the ultimate solution, goal, when it is for good, is pleased by The Divine Love.

I speak differently, because each time I, or Anyone Here requests help or hope or changes in some form, We try to get your attention so you will think of the Importance of this accomplishment occurring, helping someone you do not know, perhaps; but each time this occurs, your Soul is blessed abundantly for your generosity, for your caring, for your sincerity, and for your belief that in requesting hope, you will receive hope.

Never forget, the goodness you register that you alone speak for the betterment of something, for the good of something, you are blessed for your kindness. Never forget this."

SEPTEMBER 15, 2005 AT 1:56 P.M.

"There are Several of Us present.

It is a privilege to be where you are, because We know the sincerity that you walk in every day, and that is to help Souls of millions of human beings. Most you do not know personally, but there are many available, that *All that is delivered, put into print, will aid some or many on the Subject Matter that is of Such Great Importance* to the mentality and to the manner of how some individuals do not understand what is morally sound, morally correct, or should be applicable to how they speak, so as to leave a good memory to others they speak to.

Once an individual learns how to speak words, and through his or her personality, they are accustomed to certain circumstances, plus the company of others they know, thus making speech a common communication, and also a common manner of association.

It is Important that Words that We deliver keep you alert to what you are subjected to, because sometimes it is easy to forget, but there are Several of Us present today, and We are fully aware how Important 'speech' is amongst human beings, and how those who do not understand the language you use, oftentimes repeat in their manner of thinking and they do it using another word or words, not applicable in a proper manner.

You may ask why would I speak this way today. It is just to remind you that in your manner of life, oftentimes you may be in the company of those you know, but there may be others listening and you do not have a communication normally with them.

I smile when I say My next Words: Never forget that what you speak is very often remembered, and very often it can mean something else by the words you use, or how you speak them.

The *Gift of speech* is a Gift that leaves with others more about you and your personality, than you rarely think about, and also, do not forget, when you say your prayers, do it with dignity, and remember: **The One listening to you hears everything you say, and wants your Soul to be pure and your life at one time, to be called 'a Saint'.**"

SEPTEMBER 15, 2005 AT 2:31 P.M.

SEVERAL SAINTS

"There are Several of Us present. It is Our Privilege, Our Pleasure and Our Gift of Divine Love each time We are requested or allowed to speak Words, have Them put into script for others to read.

For the most part, human beings do not realize when they are Spiritually Blessed by The Holy Ones Here in the Heavens, because they do not feel it in a physical way, but I assure you, it is often done to give strength, more understanding, many different types of help, and of course, a Blessing to aid them to accomplish What The Father Wills them to accomplish. It can be something they are interested in, but do not have the availability to accomplish it. That is why *Prayer is oftentimes a Great Asset* to a desire, a wish, or a love that they would like to use for the good they see in it, for it, about it.

I could speak hours on the Importance of so many things that human beings are gifted with, for, and many other Words could add to this, because in the Creation of human life **so many Gifts were instilled, to allow the individual to use many Gifts that they would not know they had, until they used them,** based on a thought, a concern, or an innate desire to think about its existence that could be possible to them, to have and to use.

There are so many Words that could be spoken or put into print regarding how The Creator, in Such Just Kindness, opened many avenues for an individual human mind and body to be able to use for goodness, for a deeper understanding of the availability to aid so many areas of life, and to fulfill vacancies that would be present and not show that there could be aid, help, to make them greater than they appear to be.

Much Love goes with this Message on this day, because it is Important to know what you are capable of doing, so you can do it in the proper manner, reasonability, purpose, and goal that it has possibilities to arrive at.

The Father, in His Love for the Creation of human life, thought with Such Indepthness, Such Hope, and yes, Much Love that covered more issues than the human mentality can perceive to be. Never forget, Love from The Creator is because you are a human being."

SEPTEMBER 15, 2005 AT 3:52 P.M.

OUR HEAVENLY FATHER
MANY SAINTS

"Many of Us are present. We have been. It is always a pleasure for Us to see how you work together to supply others with Important Facts and Figures.

Today, as you take these Words, there are Thousands More that could be put into script, only because there are so many throughout the world who should know about *'This Gift'* and *What It gives Verbally, Intentionally, and to aid others in how to address Important Subjects;* because, to be created a human being has more facts of Importance in its favor than it is often seen to be, but I promise you, as you walk the way you walk, and you take part in sharing with others *a Gift of This Nature, These Facts, This Good, and This Innate Gift of Sharing Important Words, Important Facts,* giving to others the ability to one day understand that at one time, *All This occurred, and It was All in Divine Plan.*

Divine Plan is not always seen for the Beauty It is, or the Love It portrays, but Divine Plan is the Foundation for what the future will receive.

I, your Father, smile at this, and I say, 'I bless you for how you act, how you care, and what you do, what you participate in, but also, everything you say to help others more deeply understand that *there is a Higher Existence in Divine Plan that cares for every human being created throughout the world.*' Remember this. It is Important for many to understand."

SEPTEMBER 16, 2005 AT 11:12 A.M.

OUR HEAVENLY FATHER
MANY SAINTS

"*The little one* is always aware of Our Presence, and We All smile when, after she receives The Father's Love for human life, human living, she knows that We are ready to help her say Words that will give more strength on what is being practiced for the good of Souls for many, many, many other people.

This Gift, that bears so many Words, was given to encourage others to more indepthly understand *how close I am to man*.

In the design of human living, human life, a *Gift* was instilled. This *Gift* is Greater than It is understood to be, because *It is an Important Part of The Holy Trinity*. When It is ignored that Its Presence is evident, it is a great sadness to Those of Us Who understand the Importance of what *this Gift* does to, not just the Soul, but the physical being, the mentality of the human Gift of life, of living the life it was created for.

She stares at Me, for she feels the Presence of Several with Me. She has asked Me Who They are. They are Souls like the Soul you have, but These have arrived Where I Am, because of how They were lived at another time.

    She says, 'I want to cry.' We say to her, 'We understand,' because *a Blessing of this Nature, this Magnitude, this Closeness, is a Gift Beyond what the human mentality ever sees It to be, or truly understands It to be*, because It cannot be seen with the naked eye, not unless a *specific* Gift is present, at a definite chosen time by The Father Who knows how each individual loves Him.

    When We speak, We speak in Our Terminology, because it is to allow those present to more fully, indepthly understand that We have the Privilege, through Divine Will, to be places that others cannot see Us, but Our Presence is always for a purpose for The Divine.

    I will close, but I assure you, each step you take, because of how you feel, the Gift of Divine Love is Real, and It gives to you this physical, mental, and moral strength to be reminded of the *Goal* you were created to reach for your Soul. More could be spoken, but it will be at another time."

SEPTEMBER 16, 2005 AT 12:40 P.M.

OUR HEAVENLY FATHER

"I, your Heavenly Father, have used *this little one* for many years to let others understand or know about different situations that were present, and that *how they acted* was of great importance, because, very often, when incidences or situations or conditions evolve amidst other human beings, they are not always seen for their full brunt of what they are access to, capable of, or to cause in the lives of other human beings.

I smile at *this little one.* She is always exacting, even when I speak, because she worries and is concerned for one Word being out of concept of What I am Willing or Wanting others to understand.

The physical is a very important part of human life, and oftentimes, those yet in the living state ignore the importance of it.

I come today because of My Deep Love for *'This Gift'* I have given to the world. It has been in existence a long time, but the *Gift* was through *one small voice,* but *What* was behind *'The Gift'* and within *'The Gift',* was and is *Monumental in Meaning, in Concept,* and in what is expected of It by Myself, and Many Others Here in the Heavens with Me.

You live in a time where so much erratic understanding is available. People have automatically assumed that, in the change of atmosphere, and conditions of how individuals lived, and also, how individuals think, and also how individuals are educated in different phases, different facts regarding moral, immoral, just or unjust, hope or despair.

Today as I speak, it is because of My Divine Love for human life. In the Creation of it, it was to give purpose, hope, understanding and goals, giving to human lives the ability to do so many things with a purpose, for a reason, and because of Divine Love.

I could speak hours on this Subject, but I want all ages to understand, that when I give *a Gift of Communication* with an individual, it is to allow My Love, My Will, to aid and to give strength where it is needed, when it is needed, and to give hope; but also, to awaken the mentalities of so many human beings, to all the things that occur, can occur, outside of the realm in which they live or are thinking.

I will tell *the little one* What I want done with This, but as I close these Words, I have spoken Them because so many times My Words are not seen for What I deliver Them to be.

    I love human life. I created it. I gave to human life more *Gifts* than many know it to be, but I promise you, *My Love is to Want every human being to return to Me as 'a Saint' Where I am, in Heaven.*"

SEPTEMBER 16, 2005 AT 1:16 P.M.

OUR HEAVENLY FATHER

"*This Gift* I have given to the world is to draw Souls closer to Me through the ones in whom They were placed at the moment of conception.

In the creation of human living, human lives, both male and female, I have given to them responsibilities; but also, a deep understanding of the purpose in how they live, how they act, and how they associate with others like themselves, or others who are of another gender, because in the creation of human life there were so many decisions of importance, giving to human life the beauty, the wonder, and the abilities that each gender was capable of, and important in, because *it was the way it was designed to be, by The Holy Trinity.*

As I speak each time through *This Gift*, I do it with Much Love for those who partake in *This Gift*, and those who give honor to It by their willingness to share in what others will learn from *This Gift* by reading What has been put into script, but also, by learning in communicative manners, the importance of each act and each manner of addressing an important part in the human mentality, thus giving to all ages, the understanding that the human mind has the ability to instruct and to give the facts in a manner and way understandable, for the individual to use in a source, force, manner, degree, and way all things were created for.

As you look at your finger it is but a stick, but the finger can do many things by how you use it. Never forget this, and as you look at one of your feet, it is to give you the strength to stand on, and it has a purpose.

I could speak hours on end regarding the importance of how a human being is gifted with so many parts of it that mean so much to how the individual lives, how the individual can use so many things that nothing else created has the ability to do.

I will close, but before I do, I say, 'It is important to remember: *To be created a human being, you are gifted with dignity, purpose, and a hope that nothing else created is the recipient of, because in the Creation of this Gift of Divine Love, it also has a Soul that must be returned to The Creator and be called "a Saint".'"

SEPTEMBER 17, 2005 AT 10:53 A.M.

OUR HEAVENLY FATHER

"I am your Heavenly Father.

I use a small body, but a mind that loves Me more than anyone could possibly determine it to be.

I have given to the world a Blessing: First, in the Creation of human life, human living; and then, in the physical and mental abilities I instilled to give purpose and many facts of being able to identify different facets wherein the human mind would understand things that, before the Creation of human life, were not needed, were not available: the true design, and all the factors, features, fundamentals that were made to give to human living, *Gifts* that they would be exposed to, aiding their manner of life to a different role than other things created, such as the animals, the earth, and several unseen facts, factors.

I speak differently, but it is to give you a broader view on the fact that in the Design and Creation of human life, it had been given *a Goal*, to one day reach the *Goal* in a Degree to be returned to Who I Am, What I Am, for *'That Portion'* of them to be returned *pure*. It is the *'Soul'*.

I enjoy All I can speak and have put into print, thus giving to those in the living state, *motives*, *understanding*, and the *knowledge* that would give them the facts to follow, to one day return to Me and be called *'a Saint'*.

Nothing is impossible to Me. I have been given All that is needed, because of Who I Am, What I Am, and also, in being *this close* to the Creation of All Things, I understand *the Greatness it is to be created a human being, based on Divine Plan.*

I want to speak hours because there is so much I have to say, but I know there is another time, another day, and I also know *the little one* is concerned in a loving way, because of the Importance of What I have spoken. I smile at her as she looks at Me. Her love radiates for every human being created the human way."

SEPTEMBER 18, 2005 AT 10:05 A.M.

OUR HEAVENLY FATHER

"I am your Heavenly Father.

I use *one small voice, one small body* to help others understand that the size of human beings is not a definition of obeying Who I Am. Even when children say they love Me, I hear them because *My Communication is in Divine Measure, Meaning, and Purpose*. In the human way of thinking, size many times is a point of judgment. This is not wrong; but, it is as I judge human life in, on, or for.

I hold *this little one* tightly. Her response to Me is always as it should be, as this is according to What I Will to use her, for others to see and learn from What I have to say, through her, to them.

I have given to the world a rather *Unusual Blessing* from Me, because in many ways It was and is to awaken other minds to *how close I am to them*, no matter what gender, what size, or whether it is a condition, situation, or place that is My Choice to draw their attention to Me.

I smile as I speak these Words, because *Who I Am*, others would not even think I would speak like this.

The purpose for prayer to all human beings is for them *to be close to Me*, either personally when they call My Name, or through the Saints I have selected, that are with Me.

I smile when I say these Words because, for some, They may be a little difficult to accept, but *every human life created has a Goal, and that is to return to Me, Where I Am."*

SEPTEMBER 19, 2005 AT 10:57 A.M.

GOD THE FATHER

"Communication is one of the *Greatest Gifts* instilled into the Gift of human life. Without it, there would be so much confusion and wrong conception of even the moral values necessary to protect one's Soul and mentality of subject matter or physical practices of the flesh.

In My Creation of human life, I used all the assets of how a human being could understand the Importance of all that was necessary to be practiced, based on the Truth, the Logic, and the Realities that gave strength to the mentalities of what the results should be, due to the fact that human lives had to be sure that they were acting and projecting what they felt for the good of their *Soul, that is 'a Portion' of Who I Am, What I Am.*

Granted, it is not always feasible to some individuals' mentalities, to abide by what is logical, but it is a necessity that should never be overlooked, because *the Soul is the receiver of, or the victim of,* the one in whom They were placed at the moment of conception of human life.

My Intentions to request, to want to be done, is a Gift of My Divine Love to aid the mentality in the Logic, the Purpose, and the Dignity involved in how a human being should respond, not just on What I have spoken, but other facets, necessities, of dealing with the physical and mental values, gifts, and usefulness of, the necessities of, to be accomplished, of the Logic of Divine Will; thus, aiding dignity, respect, loyalty and other such actions of human living to never be dismissed, but be followed in honor and dignity, due to the fact that human life was created in respect and Divine Love, thus giving it the respect of dignity in how It serves the human life, to be a part of."

SEPTEMBER 19, 2005 AT 11:54 A.M.

OUR HEAVENLY FATHER

"I am your Heavenly Father.

Because of your sincere interest and participation in What I have given to the world, it is Important that you understand that each time you write One Word in My Name, It will represent at a later time, a greater degree of understanding because of the Importance of how human beings are beginning to more deeply comprehend that *when I speak, and as I speak, it is Obvious, My Will in What I say.*

Today I will want you to more fully, more indepthly practice your manner of prayer, because in this way of doing it, you will find it more personal, and more deeply understood where your Soul is concerned, your will is concerned, your examination to others is concerned, and your love for The Divine more in tune, helping you to think in a greater degree of communication over and above some of the formal manners and forms that you are used to. I do not belittle the formal prayers or communications with Me; in fact, I thank those who practice them to aid others in learning more.

Before I close at this time, I want you to realize that I do speak these Words because of My Sensitivity to the Importance of personal communication and what it gives to an association, thus being able to remember more indepthly, the meaning of What was spoken.

When you say a prayer that has been around a very long time, I appreciate those also, because it tells Me your Spirituality is based on not just a new idea, but the practicality of how you learned something that gave you and gives you, a communicative association in a way and manner that you do not reject but you cling to it, because you understand in the words that were spoken before and repeated again, have the chance to be remembered longer in time, than others can."

SEPTEMBER 19, 2005 AT 1:10 P.M.

OUR HEAVENLY FATHER

"I am your Heavenly Father.

It is a pleasure to speak to you, each of you, each time I am able to tell you, in some way, the Importance of what you are very concerned about.

In so many ways, when someone is loved as much as you love those who attend a hospital or sick room to give aid to someone you know, it is always blessed in a manner and way you do not know.

Today as I speak, it is to thank you for every time that you are concerned for someone you feel close to, because Prayer is an Important Item. It is a reminder to All the Saints, because it reminds Them to do what They can to support what is good for the one who is in a condition or a manner or way with some inequality to function properly, as is normal to the human way.

Prayer is a Greater Gift than it is seen or known to be. It is a Line of Communication directed, and when I hear the name or the condition or the possibilities that could arise, I assure you, I do not miss one word, but I oftentimes know some things that could cause things not to adjust as quickly as We would All like it to.

Each human being's body and mind, even though it is named with the same names of parts, places, things, circumstances, the body is sometimes a little different, and some need more help than others; but, I assure you, when you pray, your prayers are taken into consideration, because you care enough to speak them, but sometimes the body of the individual needs much deeper help, but *the prayer does give hope, and that is an Important thing for every human being created.*

Your love for The Divine is remembered at all times, and your care for those for whom you pray, it is never dismissed in any way.

I love you for all you accept and you will to be done, because, do not forget, I had a Son Who walked the human way, and He, in His Love for human life, accepted what would be possible for others to suffer at another time, another day. This Sacrifice of His was meant to be more than It shows to be. It was to remind human beings for all time to come, that to suffer in the human way, perhaps has a reason, but never forget, prayers are a great help each time you pray."

SEPTEMBER 20, 2005 AT 8:30 A.M.

OUR HEAVENLY FATHER

"We many times speak through *this little one* that is used to transfer Certain Subjects that are available for more discernment regarding Them. Most times as the Words pass through her, They are taken as natural conversation.

In the beginning of the time of *This Gift*, wherein there was so much Wording, helping other human beings to become aware of conditions, circumstances that should be looked at as being perhaps, not correct, thus to be aware of what they meant for the Soul, the body, the circumstances, and/or the reasonability of how to see what was possibly to be more satanic than humanly dramatic.

We use *a small voice*, but an obedient one. We also are aware that most human beings could not innately or intellectually or spiritually accept the Full Meaning of What We say, We project to be thought about. In most cases it is not innocence that would do this. It is most times personal understanding.

I could speak hours on all that is feasible for all ages to comprehend. The importance of each day of living the human way is a day to evaluate what one is exposed to, and for each one to associate whether a condition, a situation, or an evaluation or an interpretation of an act, of a thought, to not be seen for what it will do to the mentality and the value of how an individual partakes in the human manner of living.

I will close. We All speak so strongly through *this little one*, many times with Words not common to the human manner of thinking, and/or accepting, due to the fact of the time, or the circumstances in which they live.

There is one beautiful factor available, and that is: *I love all who are created, because there is a Goal that I have seen to be available for the Souls yet to come."*

SEPTEMBER 20, 2005 AT 11:12 A.M.

OUR HEAVENLY FATHER

"**I** am your Heavenly Father.

You live in a time wherein there is so much necessity for more in-depth understanding regarding what human beings understand is feasible, plausible and useful, but also applicable to understanding *Who I Am, and My Purpose for coming to them at this time with so much Information, Direction, and Concern for what is occurring that is not, in any way, what I Will it to be,* because It has been ignored, due to the fact that there are so many areas of human living that can easily be based on what immorality is a great part of, or superiority is so volatile in how it encourages some to perform.

I speak differently, but I speak to open the door to subjects that ordinarily are not realized as subjects to be concerned about.

I have given to the world *a Gift*, Greater than It is seen to be. I have placed It through *one small voice*, but I can also say to you, sincerely, that when I use individuals to respond to My Will, it can be in many ways, on many subjects, that include *the Souls* that are many times *the victims of* wrong actions, words, and repetitive moods.

I will close these Words at this time, because I know What I have spoken can be difficult to understand It, in Its Full Meaning to Me, but I bless those who, in their own way, try to understand how I feel in every day's manner of accepting what is *not* feasible or normal; it is only accessible."

SEPTEMBER 20, 2005 AT 12:20 P.M.

OUR HEAVENLY MOTHER

"I am your Heavenly Mother.

My Presence is because I care so Indepthly on all you do to serve in a very special way, The Heavenly Father Who loves you.

This *Gift* that has been delivered in such a Beautiful Manner and Way, is *a Gift that will one day be seen for What a Precious Gift of Divine Love It was and is.*

The little one I use to speak My Words is one that so Many of Us use, because of the Importance of Our Communication with you, and others, too.

This *Gift* is Greater than It is understood or realized to be. A Gift of This Communication, spoken privately, is basically for the whole world to see and to understand that The Creator of All Things, The Father, in Divine Ways, communicates indelibly with how He feels about human beings.

The Reason these Words are spoken today, He asks that We give thanks for Him, to you who use your time to spread What He Wills others to learn from The Divine, *the Closeness human lives have to*

All that is a Treasure of Divine Love, beyond what It is understood to be.

I close and I say, 'Your service is appreciated, but even greater than that word *"appreciate"*, it is being used to help *Your Souls* Another Way, Another Day.'"

SEPTEMBER 20, 2005 AT 12:51 P.M.

SAINT MARGARET MARY ALACOQUE

"**I** am Saint Margaret Mary Alacoque.

There are so Many of Us present, because of the Importance of What you have accepted to not just participate in, but to help in the Direction The Father Wills for others to receive What is good for their Soul, and for their manner of living in the human world.

Many children are not being instructed in the degree and manner understandable to them. Many of them would be so happy to know and to innately understand that, *in the Creation of human life there was definitely Divine Plan,* thus giving to human life so many things to aid them, to strengthen their understanding and their will to be able to more use the Important Stature of how they believed, and how well they knew about It as It being Important for their Soul.

When individuals do not feel that the younger understand certain facets that are of Importance, We try to reach them to not be so doubtful, but to use words and watch for the response, the reaction and/or the satisfaction that a younger one responds with, and to, and for, and in.

Hours could be spoken on how important it is to be example, and through example, be specific in what is morally sound, morally correct, morally feasible, morally adaptable, and yes, morally good for the Soul and for the mentality of every human being.

There is so much to be spoken on the **Importance** of human life and the **Goal** for which The Father has It waiting at a given time. What should be allowed to be known is that *no creation was not The Father's Will, because in the human manner of being a human being, there is a Goal Greater than It is seen to be.*

I beseech you, those who take the words and those who will read the Words: *Never dismiss The Divine Love, The Divine Purpose, The Divine Goal. It is always available, even though It does not show in the manner you feel would be necessary for a Goal of This Measure, This Greatness, This Divine Love."*

SEPTEMBER 20, 2005 AT 1:18 P.M.

SEVERAL SAINTS

"There are always Several of Us present wherever *this little one* is that We All use to speak Our Words so that others will understand important issues, conditions, situations, values, and the importance of living in the service to The Creator, thus helping others get to know Him more indepthly and with more assurance regarding His Presence daily.

We have used *this little one* for such a long time, knowing that What We Willed her to deliver would be done according to how It was meant to be seen, heard, felt, or known.

Throughout the world there are millions of human beings, all ages, all backgrounds, all degrees of intellects, but also, all degrees of willingness to understand that **to be created a human being is based on Divine Plan**, not human understanding, or requesting, or total ability to handle in its full value of what it is and was created to be.

In the creation of human life, it began in a very logical form of each step being a strength, or a knowledge, or a hope, or a belief in understanding the reason for **being part of this Gift that could only be of Divine Will, Design, and Purpose.**

Each decade of timing had a purpose to it, giving a step closer to what you have the privilege at this time to see in many facets of growth, allowing you at this time to have, not just responsibility, but knowledge that was not able to be given at the moment of conception of human life, human living.

A Blessing of the Major Factor you are the recipients of, is a Gift of Divine Love's Hope that with What you are conscious of, you will use It in Its Design, Its Purpose, Its Reasonability and Its Goal, because of the Souls that are involved, yours and everyone else's. Remember this. The list is endless.

I have only given you the first step, but with this first step it will give you the *strength* and the *innate understanding* that your human life, that you were gifted with at another time, *is the foundation for your Goal: to return to The Creator of All Things and have Him say to you, 'Welcome, My Saint. I have waited for you.'"*

SEPTEMBER 21, 2005 AT 11:55 A.M.

OUR HEAVENLY FATHER

"There are Many of Us present because of the Importance of so many Souls needing to learn about what it takes for them to return to The Creator and even privately be called *'a Saint'*, not always necessary for it to be an outspoken terminology, because it is like how you live today, your time in thinking is private and your association with The Creator is not always discussed with others you are with or who know you.

I smile when I say these Words through *this little one*, because each time I speak, she is so serious and Every Word she receives has an Amazing Importance to It, in It, for It.

I have given to the world *this voice*, knowing that so many created would learn so much more of the Important Factors if a *Gift like This* was allowed to be, because ordinarily, the mind and the imagination or the understanding is difficult when there are no words to hear that have a Definite Value to Them, Reason for Them, or They are given as a Gift of My Divine Love, aiding all who hear the Words, all who will speak the Words, to be stronger morally, emotionally, and yes, in their love for The Divine.

As I close these Words, I say, 'Never forget, you were created according to how it was designed to be, and you have the *Gift* of being able to understand that within you, *you have the privilege to one day return to Me in a manner and way, perhaps inconceivable to your understanding now, but the Goal never leaves you, nor does it Me.*'"

SEPTEMBER 21, 2005 AT 12:41 P.M.

"**I** am Saint Athanasius. I am Saint Agnes. I am Saint Margaret Mary Alacoque; and I am Saint Therese of Lisieux.

Many times there are Several of Us present where *this little one* is, but We offer her only one Name or two Names at the most; even though she sees More of Us present, she is obedient to Our Will and mentions only the Names she is given.

As I speak to her and through her at this time, it is to awaken the minds of those present, but also who will read What is spoken, because it is Important for it to be known that there are many things occurring in many places, even close to where you are, that should not be practiced or thought about in a manner of good, or ideal in the concept it appears to be.

You do live in a time worse than many other times in the history of human living, human lives; but, *at this time, there are so many excuses made and so much ignored,* but I assure you, your Soul is the *recipient* in ways you do not fully understand or comprehend. The *reflection* that appears within your Soul when, where you are, or who is speaking where you are, comes to light with the individual's meaning that is many times *not* what it should be.

Stories From Heaven

There are thousands of Words that could be written with Unlimited Directions; basically, because of *the Souls that can become the victims* of those who *ignore* what is right, pure, morally justifiable. Sometimes there are so many excuses all ages practice.

Thousands and thousands and thousands of Words have been put into script through this Gift, because of the Importance of the Souls that become *the victims* of those who mistreat speech, actions, thoughts even; but also, their association physically with others — some they know, and some they do not know in a personal degree, manner, way.

This Gift must be seen and heard throughout the world, due to the fact that *morality has been washed away* in words I do not want to say, and *so many excuses* are expressed in a rather personal way, but the subject matter is demeaning to the Soul of those present and those who will hear the words spoken.

I could speak hours on this subject, because in many ways, it is *diabolical*, but many do not want to see what they call 'humor' as being so diabolical they should not partake in it.

As I close these Words at this time, I do it with My Love for The Divine, and My Desire to help millions of human beings more indepthly understand, that if they partake in what is immoral, impure and negligent for them to even think about — I am sorry, I must stop now. I have tears, because I could speak hours in trying to convince Divine Concern for human man."

SEPTEMBER 21, 2005 AT 1:30 P.M.

"There are always Many of Us present where *this little one* is, because The Father has requested that We take Words and put Them into print so others will enjoy What This Gift is all about, and the Importance of It through *one small voice.*

There is no human being alive that does not need **This Script** that has so much Meaning in It, so much Reason for It, and gives to a human being the Support that is sometimes necessary to aid one in many different types of circumstances that appear in human living.

Today as I speak, I speak with Much Love, because to be created a human being has much more Worth than it is seen to have, because in the Creation of human life, there are *Gifts* beyond what are understood to be, because the human mind cannot see the *Gifts* and cannot always perceive *the Importance of such Gifts* that were designed to be in human living, and some to last beyond that time and be present if the individual was announced to be 'a Saint'.

The **Goal** for human life is far more than It is understood to be. ***It is a Future, Planned by The Creator, thus giving it a manner to communicate what it was committed to be, a Soul close to The***

Creator forever and ever and ever. What more could an individual ask?

The Father loves human life and in His Design of it, His Planning for it, He didn't miss one thing because of His Love for what this stands for, and that is to be in Heaven for All Eternity."

SEPTEMBER 21, 2005 AT 1:50 P.M.

SAINT ANGELA MERICI

"**I** am Saint Angela Merici.

So many of Us Saints are attentive where you are, because of your concern and your sincerity in how you apply, protect, and accept the Importance of the *privilege* you have been given by The Heavenly Father, because most times, when an individual hears of a Saint, unless something has been put into script applicable to different reasonings, practices, ways of the Saint, very little can be understood.

Today you live in a time when it is important that so many Saints be understood by different facts, conditions, and situations that They are accountable for in an open way, because what They sacrifice, and what part They play or take in aiding The Heavenly Father by submitting different facts that are important for those yet in the living state to more deeply understand that, *as a Saint, there are many things that can by taken care of, for reasons understandable to Those Here in the Heavens.*

Needless to say, so Many of Us could speak hours, but We have been requested to put things into script that will give, perhaps the Groundwork, or Different Subjects that will be practical for others to learn more indepthly, believing in *Sainthood as the Goal for life.*"

SEPTEMBER 21, 2005 AT 2:09 P.M.

"**I** am a Priest. I will not further My Information on this, because I want My Words to be What is Important for the Souls of millions of human beings.

Every human being created **has a Goal to reach for 'That Portion' within it that is 'a Portion of The Creator'**. Human life was created to use human life as the means to a Greater Way, Source of Service to The Creator in a Very Beautiful Way.

When a Saint is announced as having reached a Definite Standard of Importance, there is a need for others to know that this time in His or Her life has much responsibility and much demand for The Creator to use, to aid where it is necessary and to give strength when it is needed, but also, *to serve for the betterment to reach the Goal*.

My next Words are sad, only because not all human beings realize that *there is a Goal for 'That Portion' of them that is to return to The Creator*, and be aware that service developed when the time came for that Soul to do The Father's Will in degrees, manners, and ways that would serve, aid, and maybe even counsel Souls that needed this added System, Condition, so the Soul would be able to be used by The Creator at a time that would give other Souls strength, hope, and add to their manner of doing things, what The Father would use as *a tool*.

I could speak hours, but I know that My Words may confuse some individuals, but there is nothing to be confused about, not when there is so much Divine Love, Divine Hope, Divine Care, and All the things that help give to the Soul strength to follow The Father's Will, beyond what it is known to be by the human race of those who still have the ability to perceive many Important Things; because, do not forget, **the Love of The Divine is Far Beyond what the human love of human life can perceive It to be."**

SEPTEMBER 22, 2005 AT 9:55 A.M.

OUR HEAVENLY FATHER

"I speak often through *one small voice*, because I am assured she will transfer to others What I Will her to speak.

You live in a time wherein *Prayer* is not always seen for the *Importance* it is. These times must change.

Today, as I speak through *one small voice*, My Reason is to alert others to My Presence, and that I do hear what they will Me to hear when they draw My Attention to them. My Divine Love is obviously aware at all times regarding all created for that *Precious Goal* that was made for them to return to and be with Me, in a different Way and Manner than they now live in the human form.

Children are not being instructed enough on the fact that prayer is a communication unseen, but all prayers are heard, I promise you this.

Today as I speak, it is to give strength and an understanding of *how close I am to all human beings*. Do not forget, you have a *Soul, 'a Portion' of Who I Am, What I Am,* and the Soul is the *recipient* of everything you think, do or practice. The *Soul* you bear is *a Gift of*

Divine Love to assure you, you are never out of any distance with your communication with Me, with Who I Am.

I will close these Words at this time. *Do not forget What I have just spoken from The Divine.*"

SEPTEMBER 22, 2005 AT 12:20 P.M.

"**W**ords that should be indelibly marked in the mentalities of all human beings, should be understood as the *foundation* for correct answers, correct participations, and correct abilities to participate in what would be morally sound, correct, right.

The word *'maybe'* has much appearance in many areas of life. The words *'could be'* also have much attention, because they give a general view for decision. The words are endless, because wording puts an *emphasis* on what most individuals stress for how they want what they are speaking or writing or delivering words that would aid what they will others to know, to accept.

The little one I speak through and to, oftentimes angers when there are words that, in their very activity, stress obscenities, indignities, imperfections, and raw understanding of what should be spoken instead.

You live in a time where there are many variations of the meaning of certain words that are used in what I would call *an abundant way*, because it seems to capture a stronger view for the one speaking, and the one wanting to impress a meaning.

I know I speak differently at this time, but it is important to follow what is meant to be correct and in good sense. So much is going on that so many are using wrong in how they address conditions, places, situations and, of course, their opinions.

I want to speak long, but I know that I will be able to come back at another time, because What I have just spoken disturbs *the little one* so Many of Us use on Important Issues, Statements, Evaluations, and many More such as These represent."

SEPTEMBER 22, 2005 AT 1:18 P.M.

SAINT ANTHONY OF PADUA

"**I** am Saint Anthony of Padua.

I have requested The Father for My Privilege to speak to all of you who work for Him, helping Him to deliver to more people, **the Important Goal for which human life was created.**

The little one has tears. They are Mine, because as I speak, I speak with Much Love for those who spend their time in service to The Divine, thus able to deliver to so many human beings, so Many Lessons, and so Much Divine Love to be held as a Favor from The Divine.

To most individuals, the word *'Divine'* does not mean what It really means in Concept, in Definition, and in Its Purpose. Words oftentimes are not seen for the Greatness They are, for individuals to feel the reasonability for these Words to be spoken, thus *adding to What is being delivered, the closeness these Words are to The Heavenly Creator and All Those with Him Who share, in many ways, What He Declares to be Important for Souls of All Dimensions.*

Children should be enlightened on how Important it is to be born a human being, thus *having the privilege* to one day return to

The Creator of All Things, be with Him and with The Heavenly Mother, in a Manner and Way Comfortable, and that bears Much Happiness that no other place could they receive.

I know I speak differently, but it is to express Our Love for those who participate in learning so much and in participating in certain facets of activity that give strength in so many ways, and sometimes monetarily.

To be created a human being is a *Gift* beyond what it is known or seen to be, because it is not seen in all that it consists of: First of all, **the conception is Blessed by The Holy Trinity**; and then, from then on, there are different degrees of time, giving to the conception more time to be seen as what comes naturally to age at a later date; also, all the facets of advancement physically, mentally, socially, and many other things.

We All smile at these Words, because *human life is so special.* If it were not so *special*, why would The Creator have come at a time a long time ago, and used the *special form of a human body* to walk amidst others, speak and teach them things they did not know? You call It **'The Father, The Son and The Holy Spirit.'** The Names are Beautiful, but all that has preceded this time that you live, has been One Beautiful Gift of Divine Love after Another.

You live in a time where the sensitivities to what is right over what is wrong, what is good over what is evil, what is pure over what is impure, what is just over what is unjust, are the Most Beautiful Gifts to live by, with, for and in, because Each One proclaims a Greatness, an Importance, and a Beautiful Gift of Divine Love.

I will close, but as I do, I say, 'The Father loves those who look to Him and pray, but He also is grateful when Others are prayed to, because *in The Heavenly Way, there is a Unification of Souls* that nothing else has.' The Souls are Gifts of Divine Love, above and beyond what the human mentality can perceive to be.

Always remember: *Being created a human being is a Gift of Divine Love with a Goal, and that is to return to from Where It came as a Soul.*"

SEPTEMBER 23, 2005 AT 9:57 A.M.

OUR HEAVENLY FATHER

"I am telling *this little one* not to worry so much. I am always available to aid her in what she is so capable of accomplishing.

Love in the human way of living differs than I, in My Love for human life. In the Creation of human life, there is Much Respect, Much Concern, and Much Divine Love that oftentimes is the Salvation of things that occur, not always feasible to the human mind.

This Gift the world has been presented with, is Far Above what the human mentality or ability could perceive It to be.

Many times I smile at those who question the degree of obedience they should be inclined to follow. I will say it this way: *An innate love for The Divine is logical*; this list is endless, because in the Creation of human life, there was a Beautiful Purpose, and a Sharing beyond what It can or could be understood as, or in Its Full Measure.

The Gift of human life is that *step* to a Greater Way for the human mind to one day see it in a different degree and obvious manner for living."

SEPTEMBER 23, 2005 AT 11:55 A.M.

OUR HEAVENLY FATHER

"This Blessing of My Divine Love, that I use one small individual to dictate My Will, My Love, My Words, for others to be able to understand *My Presence is Real and My Love for them Divine.*

I come in this manner and way to allow What I want others to know, that there is a *Goal* for *'That Life'* that they were given a long time ago. It began for a reason to thousands of human beings. It is a Gift of Divine Love, not just based on the human means.

As I speak today, I do it because I want to be with you in person, and this is the way I can do it for you to be able to handle My Presence and take My Words.

The world has been blessed abundantly at the times that others did not see it as a Blessing. When The Son of The Creator walked the earth, His Willingness to suffer was far greater than it was seen to be, because when something is Important for the Souls of human beings, it seems to be different than when it is just to help someone who is ill physically.

The little one I use, I have used for a very long time, and today, as the Words I Will you to have, I pass through her because *it is important to you to begin to understand the Importance of Divine Will, Divine Love, Divine Hope, but also, Divine Generosity.*

No human being is created without a Soul. No human being understands what *a Valuable Gift* This is, but that is why We have allowed so Many Saints to speak, and that is why I speak, because the Soul is to be returned *'a Saint'*."

SEPTEMBER 23, 2005, APPROXIMATELY 12:00 NOON

OUR HEAVENLY FATHER

"I could think of no better way to bless the creation of human life, so *each human being that is created has 'a Portion' of What I Am, Who I Am within them*, and the time will come, and that is why Heaven is so Important, for people to strive for their Soul, so the Soul can return to Heaven immediately.

When I show the Soul, because it would be impossible for anyone to draw the Soul in the way It really looks, and so the Soul can only be talked about, but one day It will be seen, and It will surprise everyone at Its Appearance, because the Soul is My Love for human life, when the time comes for It to show."

SEPTEMBER 23, 2005 AT 2:23 P.M.

OUR HEAVENLY MOTHER

"I am your Heavenly Mother.

When The Heavenly Father decided that there should be help for those in the living state, that are to one day become *Saints* Here in the Heavens, there would probably be needed Something causing attention to what the foundation, and then the purpose for this place you live in would be necessary to fulfill in a degree and manner logical, beneficial, and in many ways strength for the mental, moral, physical, social, and spiritual needs of human beings of all ages, all backgrounds, all intellects, and yes, all sensitivities, according to what The Creator would want them to have, *to give them the strength to fulfill the Goal of their one day meeting with The Creator as 'a Saint'*.

You live in a time wherein there is much differences in opinions, differences in obligations, and differences in moral views, practices, understanding, and values, but these things should not detour anyone from looking at what was requested by The Heavenly King, The Father, The Creator of All Things.

I will speak more, but there is so much to be looked at and into, to make steps that give strength to the conditions necessary to be accomplished for not just the *safety* of millions of Souls, but the *hope* that the Souls innately have, because *They know that to become 'a Saint' is the Highest Gift a human being can arrive at in Heaven.*"

SEPTEMBER 24, 2005 AT 11:13 A.M.

OUR HEAVENLY FATHER

"I am your Heavenly Father.

I have given to the world a *Gift*, Greater than they understand It to be. I have spoken so many times, and Others Here with Me have delivered Words to aid other human beings in points of personal communication with All Saints available every moment of every day.

The little one looks at My Face and she says to Me, 'I see You different today.' I smile at this statement, because she is constantly concerned that All Things that pass through her are of The Divine Word, delivered by Those Who have the *privilege* to speak through The Holy Trinity.

It is not easy to walk as she walks, speak as she speaks, because she does not hear sounds from Us. We use other means.

Each day is a day of progress for the Souls of those in the living state, because each day Many Saints Here in the Heavens speak, wanting Their Words to give Strength, Hope, and a stronger mode, manner of living the human way.

We All smile at her statement that she repeats to you, because she checks Every Word We use, always wanting It to be easily understood by those present. Her protection is a joy to see.

When *Prayer* was created, it was to give to human beings a communicative means to speak to Us at any time of the day or night. It was given to make all human beings aware that each human being can communicate every moment of every day, but also, to remind them that *their Soul, that is 'a Portion' of The Creator of All Things, receives Grace, Spiritual Love from The Divine, for partaking in the 'act of relationship' that gives strength, hope.* The Words are endless in number, what can be accomplished at different times.

We All smile when We are able to speak through *one* such as she is, has been chosen for, because it gives strength and a deeper understanding of the Reality of Our Presence with those who pray words, and also those who, at different times, ask for aid, for help from The Divine.

We would like to speak hours, because of the *Treasure of Our Communication*, to Us and the ones that receive. As the Words close in sound, I have one more thing to say: *Spiritual Strength is the Greatest Strength that a human being can be gifted with. It is based on Divine Love for all portions of human life."*

SEPTEMBER 25, 2005 AT 10:18 A.M.

OUR HEAVENLY FATHER

"I am your Heavenly Father.

It should surprise no one regarding how I choose certain individuals to do what I request them to do, no matter what it is.

I hold *the little one* tightly, because the Power I use is inconceivable to be understood in Their Full Measure, because I speak in a Manner and Way in which I try to reach all mentalities, and all degrees of abilities to understand My Manner of doing things that oftentimes cause Me to be physically present, thus announcing My Presence openly.

I have delivered Much based on My Divine Love for humanity, thus using Words understandable to aid their Souls *in My Close Association*; thus, not being able to be misunderstood regarding how I sometimes choose one individual for the time I am present, to deliver What I Will others to learn, to accept, and/or to use, *basing the Value on My Close Association at a given time with them,* so they will remember, I am not always so far out of closeness to them.

I will hold *the little one* tightly, because My Power is difficult for her small body to withstand, but I do smile at this, because she told Me not to worry, and I am letting her know I will follow what she has requested of Me. I love her and she loves Me. *The Gift of Divine Love is Greater than It is understood to be.*"

SEPTEMBER 26, 2005 AT 11:12 A.M.

OUR HEAVENLY FATHER
AND MANY SAINTS

"There are Many of Us present at different times where *this little one* is that The Father chose for many tasks to be accomplished for the benefit of Souls. She was chosen a long time ago, so is well aware of the responsibilities she endures through her behavioral understanding with The Heavenly Father, Who wants all human beings to recognize that *the Purpose for which human life was created, was given a Goal Greater than It was understood to be.*

Throughout the world there are millions of human beings who need to know about *This Gift* that has been given to the world, to be able to be read on Facts, Features, that instill into the mentalities who read Them, how Important it is for everyone to more fully understand that *in the Creation of human lives there was a Purpose, there is a Purpose, based on Divine Plan*, giving to human lives the support needed to back what they think, speak and do, when it is obviously necessary, practical, reasonable, due to the fact that *the Soul is the recipient* of everything that a human being has the privilege of partaking in.

Some who read these Words will find Them different than I usually speak, but there are so many human beings of all backgrounds, all ages, that need to learn more about Me.

I will close at this time, but I assure you, I will return, because *every human being created is gifted with 'a Portion' of The Creator.* Nothing could be more Important than this *Gift* from The Divine."

Stories From Heaven

SEPTEMBER 26, 2005 AT 12:00 NOON

OUR HEAVENLY FATHER

"**I** am your Heavenly Father.

It is a pleasure for Me to meet with you when I am able to meet with you in person.

You live in a time wherein so many individuals believe in their being *a Divine Entity of Living*, but they do not practice the necessities to honor such a Gift of My Divine Love.

To be created a human being contains so many *Gifts*: the *senses*, and *the abilities to use the mentality* to grow morally, mentally, physically, spiritually, in so many concepts of giving to human living so many more abilities to use, to one day arrive Here in the Heavens and be called *'a Saint'*.

As I close My Words, I do it with Much Love, to be able to speak as I do to those who will print the Words so others can read the Words and, *hopefully, be awakened to What is Truth.*

I love you for your dedication and for how you serve, because in your service, you are allowing so much to be learned. I bless you and I say, 'It is through those like you that many will more indepthly understand *My Existence is Fact, Truth, and Definitely Love for human living.*'"

SEPTEMBER 26, 2005 AT 12:43 P.M.

"*The little one* is with Me. It is a Sacrifice Greater than It is seen to be, because of the Importance of How I Speak and How I Deliver What should be Over and Above What others want in the manner, way they would perceive It to be.

There are so many *Gifts* that are passed through this Divine Love, that are Above and Beyond the human imagination, or ability to perceive *a Gift of This Measure, This Hope and Service*, that is instructed to be a Great Part for the human way, for the Soul to come one day to Where We Are.

I will close My Words. I know I have spoken rapidly, but sometimes *time is of Great Importance*, even to Those of Us Who work for The Divine."

SEPTEMBER 26, 2005 AT 2:06 P.M.

OUR HEAVENLY FATHER

"It is I Who have asked you if you would write. I am your Heavenly Father.

So many times when you gather and much is spoken about, I am present along with Many Others Who share with Me, the Heavens.

This Statement might be difficult for some who read It to understand My Words, the Way I have just put Them, announcing to you Certain Facts.

A *Blessing* is often thought about as just *a Spiritual Gift*. It is that, but It is also a *Gift* to give an individual strength: physical, moral, mental. It is also a *Gift* to give others who know you, the assistance or the ability to see things in a straightforward manner, based on Fact, but also, Purity in What It speaks, what It addresses morally, mentally, physically, spiritually.

I have given to the world *a Gift* through *one small voice*, but *This Gift* is to draw others to It, so they too will share in *This Gift* mentally, morally, spiritually and physically, helping others to reach out and find *the path to Heaven*. The *path* is never hidden. *It waits for all human beings to one day walk the path and be 'a Saint'.*

I speak differently, I know, but I do it because I care so much about your Souls; but never think that it is just your Soul that I care about. I care about how you think, and what your wishes and goals are, for you to one day make that trip to Where I Am, and that you will have earned the Title, 'Saint'."

SEPTEMBER 27, 2005 AT 11:47 A.M.

MANY SAINTS

"There are Many of Us present and I add to this, it is because of the Importance of human life. In its Creation, it was a Gift of Divine Love. There are so many things that are important as a human being walks in the daily way: First of all, self-care; but then the other things each have an importance to them, according to what they are committed to: physical or mental or spiritual conditions, situations, or human relations.

I know I always speak on Subject Matter that most who hear Me are not thinking about, but I want you to always remember: *Divine Love, The Creator's Love, is One that wants to give strength to every human being on many subjects, for many reasons, and in many ways.*

To be created a human being does not mean that there is not an Importance to it, in it or for it. *It has a Goal Greater than It is ever thought to truly be.*

As I close these Words, I say, 'When We are requested, or when I request Others to speak, I do it with The Love of The Creator, because no matter Who We Are or How We are addressed in Importance, it is a privilege to speak the Words that are Words Far Beyond what any human being would be able to repeat, unless of course, We are given the privilege to speak Them for others to learn from Them.' ***Divine Love is never weak.***"

SEPTEMBER 27, 2005 AT 12:16 P.M.

OUR HEAVENLY FATHER

"I am your Heavenly Father.

I come on this day for a Purpose, a Reason for you to more fully understand that to walk the *path* I chose *this little one* to walk, takes more strength, energy, obedience in service to Divine Plan.

To some, they look at It in a manner and way as it being totally a pleasure, a privilege, and a Gift Greater than human words can say, but I speak today on a very Important Subject, and that is because of the Importance that passes through *one small body, one small voice.*

It takes more than physical strength to comply with the Will of The Divine. Each sheet of Words that is delivered takes more than energy to write. *It takes strength to repeat What you cannot hear, What you cannot feel, and the Subject Matter is different than you or anyone else would place It in, a Degree Understandable to all who will read It, all who will follow It, and all who understand the Importance of It.*

My Words are harsh, but I say it because of the Importance in Every Word We speak, every time We request someone to follow What We Will. Divine Will is not like the human will. Divine Will has a different Type of Strength, Purpose and Manner of Speech.

As I close My Words, I will add: I appreciate all who serve the position they have allowed to be, using their time and energy, but I also remind you, that to be the *victim of service* takes more than energy. I could speak hours on this Subject, because It is of Great Importance for human beings to know, to understand, that to walk in The Light of The Divine, many times takes a toll in more ways than can be seen."

SEPTEMBER 27, 2005 AT 1:24 P.M.

OUR HEAVENLY MOTHER

"I am your Heavenly Mother.

I come to be with you today because I understand your values, your concerns, your interests, and how you consider morality over immorality, hope over despair, and kindness over selfishness or despair.

The world has been blessed abundantly by The Heavenly King. His Desire was for all things to be accomplished for the good they were designed for, the importance they were to human beings.

You live in a time wherein so much resistance, rejection is caused to The Divine. *The Divine is not seen always for the Greatness It Is, the Purpose It Is.*

As you walk each hour of every day, and you partake in all things that surround you, do you not think of what some of these things could cause to you? I am sure you do, because *to be a human being has an 'innate understanding'* of what is right over what is wrong, just over unjust, hope over despair, but kindness over what would be called a lack of generosity, a lack of sound communication, and a lack of being able

Stories From Heaven

to share in an ordinary or generous manner, something that you care about. This list is endless in so many ways, so many degrees. Pages of paper could be filled with just the Wording.

    I will close My Words at this time, because What I have delivered is because I, your Heavenly Mother, can sincerely say, 'I love you for what you want to have your life be responsible to, for, about, and there are so many things that oftentimes come in to try to make you make a mistake.'

    I will close, but as I do, never forget: *The Heavenly Father loves you. I, too, love you. Remember this.*"

SEPTEMBER 27, 2005 AT 2:00 P.M.

OUR HEAVENLY FATHER

"I am your Heavenly Father.

I smile when I say My next Words: Your generous act of serving an Important Fact is beautiful to see, because it shows service to The Heavenly Father in a loving way, manner, degree, that does not happen as often as it could be.

My Words are Sincere and My Love Divine. I bless you from The Heavens and I say, 'Each time you take the time to serve for the betterment of many things to be, I thank You from My Heart and want you to remember, I do love you in My Way.'"

INDEX

GOD THE FATHER 3, 5, 19, 28, 32, 34, 39, 49, 51, 53, 58, 68, 72, 78, 80, 82, 87, 96, 99, 101, 108, 116, 128, 132, 133, 135, 136, 139, 141, 145, 150, 155, 158, 160, 164, 173, 175, 177, 180, 182, 184, 186, 188, 190, 192, 194, 202, 213, 220, 221, 223, 226, 229, 231, 233, 236, 240, 244

OUR HEAVENLY MOTHER 25, 67, 72, 99, 113, 123, 137, 152, 196, 224, 242

OUR LORD 104

SAINT JOSEPH, THE HOLY SPIRIT 126

THE HOLY TRINITY 119

SAINT AGNES 204

SAINT ALPHONSUS LIGUORI 17, 45, 145

SAINT ANGELA MERICI 209

SAINT ANTHONY MARY CLARET 1

SAINT ANTHONY OF PADUA 217

SAINT ATHANASIUS 204

SAINT BERNADETTE 45

SAINT CATHERINE OF SIENA 10, 65, 90, 110, 121

SAINT FRANCIS OF ASSISI 45

SAINT MARGARET MARY ALACOQUE 30, 45, 198, 204

PADRE PIO 45

SAINT THERESE OF LISIEUX 204

SAINT(S) UNNAMED 7, 9, 12, 13, 15, 19, 22, 23, 25, 26, 28, 36, 38, 39, 41, 43, 47, 53, 56, 60, 62, 70, 72, 75, 76, 85, 92, 94, 106, 110, 130, 133, 143, 148, 152, 155, 162, 166, 169, 171, 173, 175, 200, 207, 211, 215, 231, 235, 238